I0149988

GULLIBLE'S TRAVAILS
BY
JAMES KENNEDY

Copyright© James Kennedy
ALMAFI PRESS
ISBN 978-1-9164151-0-2

CHAPTER ONE

The village of Marston consists of a green surrounded by picturesque thatched houses; mainly occupied by well to do out comers. Like many rural hamlets the original dwellers seem to have melted away into the surrounding countryside or more often drifted to nearby towns as the price of local housing continues to rise above their limited means. The postman George Mears still delivered the mail on a bicycle and this particular morning he arrived at the Colonel's gate.

Propping his bike against the manicured privet hedge, he opened the gate and hurried down the drive. The sight that met his eyes as he approached the house brought him to a sudden stop. There on the step was the Colonel; sprawled on his back staring with sightless eyes at the sky with a neat round hole in his forehead accentuated by a ring of black powder. It was not the first dead body George had seen; he had served in the infantry during the Second World War under 'Monty' in the desert campaigns then through Italy.

He dropped his delivery sack and went forward to examine the body. The old man was definitely dead; just the one shot had dispatched him and judging by the powder burn it had been fired from close quarters. The Colonel's clothes were damp from the heavy dew that morning; indicating that he had been shot some time before dawn. George straightened up and went to the phone box on the green to report to the local police.

CHAPTER TWO

By the time Cooper arrived at the scene there was a small crowd of 'rubber necks' on the Green being kept back by the local Constabulary. He made his way to the front of the house where the Forensic team was still working.

Dr.Merryweather straightened up and turned to greet him; 'Pretty straight forward Dan; shot at close quarters, time of death somewhere around twelve last night.' 'Who is he?' He looks like someone important Responded Cooper.

'Local Bigwig and War Time Hero apparently,' replied the Pathologist irreverently.

Cooper knelt down by the body and studied the scene; 'There are no marks to indicate a struggle on the path; it's probable that he knew whoever killed him.' 'No sign of a bullet case I suppose?' Merryweather grimaced; 'I just examine the stiffs; your lot is supposed to do the sleuthing.' Cooper stood up and brushed the dirt off his knees; 'when can I have your report Charles?'

'When I've finished it;' said Merryweather with mock severity; 'you blokes always want things yesterday; the dead can't be hurried you know.'

Cooper reached inside his coat for a cigarette; then thought better of it as a picture of a reproving Sheila came into his mind. She had asked him to give them up six months ago and so far he had managed; but there were times when the temptation was overwhelming.

He walked over to where the sergeant in charge of the inquiry was talking to a local man;

Cooper asked who the dead man was; 'Why it's Colonel Farrington Wells the local MP;' said the Sergeant, 'he was liked by everybody.'

'Not everybody, said Cooper, otherwise he wouldn't be lying on his doorstep with a hole in his head.'

'He was a very brave man;' said the local indignantly; a bespectacled, earnest sort of fellow; 'he led a raid on Rommel's headquarters during the war and was awarded the Military Cross.'

'Was he now;' murmured Cooper thoughtfully, 'had he any enemies that you know of?'

The man looked astonished; 'enemies? He had no enemies; why he was a Pillar of Society spending his life working for the community; people loved him.'

'Perhaps a colleague from the war had a grudge and decided to avenge it?' suggested Cooper;' someone, somewhere hated him enough to kill him'

Nodding to the sergeant Cooper made his way back to his car; he would come back to the village and make enquiries later when things had quietened down.

He arrived back at Bethel Street and went up to his office where Foley, his assistant was demolishing a cheese sandwich.

'Doesn't your landlady feed you Foley?' Cooper remarked, 'there is a time for eating and a time for work; what have you got for me?'

When Foley had swallowed enough of his mouthful to be intelligible he replied; 'Mr. Merryweather asked you to ring him, there has been a development.'

Cooper got through to the pathologist; 'what have you found Charles?'

'When I unclenched his right hand I found a white feather

in it,' Merryweather replied.

'I thought that sort of thing went out with the First World War;" said Cooper; Ladies of the time would hand them to men who had not volunteered for the Front.'

'It seems someone was determined to tell the world that the Colonel was a coward;' remarked Merryweather.

'Well it certainly supplies us with a motive,' said Cooper, 'it smacks of a military style execution so it's in that region that I shall have to start.'

CHAPTER THREE

With the help of the librarian Cooper managed to access a biography written about the Colonel's exploits. Sitting in the reading section of the library he commenced to search through the book for information about the man himself.

James, Sebastian, Farrington Wells was born in Wales to a well to do family; there was a photograph of them standing in a typical Edwardian pose. Cooper noticed that the father had a forbidding expression; there was obviously not much of the 'milk of human kindness' in that face. The mother was a handsome woman, but there was an air of sadness, almost fear in her expression. Farrington Wells Senior was a successful barrister with a flourishing practice in Swansea.

Young Farrington Wells was sent off to Boarding School as soon as he was of an age and lost his mother two years later.

It seemed that his father preferred the boy to continue to board at school and rarely bothered with him. James became interested in things military when he joined the school's Cadet Force and this led to him joining the Army on leaving.

He was too young to see action as the Armistice was declared whilst he was doing his officer training. However he was seconded to the Durham Light Infantry in Cologne during the Allied occupation where he gained a reputation as a bright and reliable Lieutenant and in due course was promoted to Captain. Two years later he was posted to India and served with distinction during skirmishes in the Kyber Pass. He became involved in Information gathering within the Pashtoon tribes of Afghanistan, in whose language he became fluent. This entailed risky sorties into tribal areas in disguise in order to glean information regarding uprisings or friction amongst the various factions. It did not take him long to climb the greasy pole of promotion and by 1935 he was a Major. Cooper paused, setting down the book; for the life of him he could not see why someone should accuse this man of cowardice, it just didn't add up. He picked up the book and went to the check out desk; he borrowed it for a couple of weeks so he could continue to look for any clues that would lead him to a suspect. In the afternoon he drove back to Marston; parking his car he proceeded to do a house to house inquiry. The first house, called 'Dunroamin' was occupied by an elderly couple named Wallace who had retired to Marston after running a successful boarding house in Great Yarmouth. They painted a glowing picture of the Colonel, saying that he was always willing to help people with a problem either in his capacity as their MP or just as a caring neighbour. When Cooper asked if they knew of anyone who did not think that he was the best thing since sliced bread, they became quite indignant.

'The man was a Saint and a public benefactor, nothing was too much trouble;' protested Mr.Wallace.

'He would always go out of his way to help people,' declared Mrs. Wallace; 'that was the sort of person he was.'

Cooper realised that he was getting nowhere with this line of questioning and changed tack.

'Did either of you notice anything unusual last night, particularly around midnight?'

Mr. Wallace thought for a moment and said; 'As a matter of fact now that you mention it there was a noise like a car backfiring and I went to the front door; but I didn't see a vehicle so I came back indoors as it had turned quite chilly.'

'That was probably the shot that you heard Mr.Wallace;' said Cooper dryly; he stood up, thanked them for their time and let himself out.

He spent the next two hours going from house to house getting pretty much the same response; according to the villagers Farrington Wells should have had a halo and a pair of wings!

CHAPTER FOUR

When he got home he took the biography to bed and continued to read James Sebastian's life story. It certainly made a good read; when the Second World War broke out Farrington Wells was posted once more, this time to Egypt where he became the Aid de Camp to Brigadier Bullingham; one of Wavell's advisors. As the campaign against the Africa Corps developed it became glaringly obvious that Rommel was continuously out thinking the British High Command.

As he advanced steadily towards Tobruk it was decided that drastic action was required and a plan to assassinate him was formulated. Farrington Wells was put in command of a group assigned for the job and they were trained secretly and then readied for action. They did not have to wait long as intelligence reports indicated that Rommel had made his headquarters at a Mansion four miles outside Sidi Barani.

The place had belonged to a French diplomat who had departed hurriedly for France when the Afrika Corps arrived! There was a small garrison protecting it and it was only a couple of hundred metres from the sea. Farrington Wells and his force were put aboard a submarine which took them up the coast from Alexandria and they went ashore in inflatable boats. They made their way through an olive grove to the wall which ran around the Mansion where two guards were overpowered and silently killed. Moving on to the house they entered through a side door and quickly spread out to search for Rommel. Unfortunately, what they didn't know was that he wasn't there; he had been recalled to Berlin to confer with Hitler.

They were discovered and a running fire fight ensued; by this time the garrison had been alerted. The group withdrew giving a good account of them selves; but they were hopelessly outnumbered and began taking heavy casualties.

Only three managed to make it back to the beach and were picked up by the submarine; Farrington Wells was not amongst them. He and two of his men were captured and interrogated before being sent to a POW camp in Biserta.

A month later he staggered in to a British forward position with several days' growth of beard, sunstroke and an amazing story of his escape. Apparently he had hidden under the camp refuse truck, hanging on to the chassis as it drove out of the camp on its way to the local dump. Then he had made his way through the desert navigating by the stars, traveling by night and hiding by day. He was sent back to Cairo for de-briefing and kitted out with a new uniform; then he was offered a position with the Long Range Desert Group which was just being formed at that time. Cooper put the book down and yawned; Sheila stirred and murmured something unintelligible, he reached out and switched off the bedside light.

CHAPTER FIVE

Next morning Cooper was sent for by Inspector Grant; 'What progress are you making on this murder in Marston Cooper?' he asked, 'I have had a call from the 'Met.' asking if you need assistance.'

'As you are no doubt aware the victim was no ordinary person, being both a War Hero and an MP.'

'I will expect your best endeavours in this case Cooper otherwise I shall accept their offer.'

'There has been pressure from Whitehall to expedite the investigation as quickly as possible in case this was the start of a vendetta against politicians in general.'

Cooper thought to himself that such a campaign would have his wholehearted support.

He said; 'I'm making some progress sir, at the moment it is a matter of tracking down possible suspects; we have little to go on at the moment.'

Grant looked over his rimless glasses and said; 'I don't want excuses Cooper, I want results; I shall expect a daily report on my desk; now if you will excuse me I have a meeting to attend at City Hall.'

Cooper left Grant's office fuming at the summary dismissal and cavalier treatment Grant always showed to him.

His track record in solving cases in Norfolk and beyond was without parallel and he resented the attitude of this bureaucratic copper.

As he entered his office Foley was looking bright eyed and bushy tailed; Morning Guv' I have some good news for you.'

Cooper sighed wearily; 'what is it Foley, has the murderer given himself up?'

'No Guv, be reasonable; we've had a phone call from some old dear who claims she used to work for the Farrington Wellses.'

He handed Cooper a slip of paper with the telephone number and name of the caller.

Cooper rang the number and asked if he was speaking to Miss Marigold Bird.

The voice at the other end of the phone sounded remarkably sprightly; 'Yes that's right officer, to whom am I speaking?'

He gave his name and rank; 'I believe you have some information for us madam?'

'Yes, I was in service for many years with the family and I was shocked to learn of Colonel Farrington Well's murder.'

'May I come and see you Miss Bird?' asked Cooper.

'Of course Detective Sergeant; if there is any help I can give you it would be the least I can do for the poor gentleman.'

Cooper took a note of her address and arranged to call on her at two that afternoon.

He arrived outside Miss Bird's terrace house in the outskirts of Norwich; it was one of many built for workers in the Victorian era.

There were flowers in the postage stamp of a garden in front of the house and the place had a neat and cared for look about it.

He rang the doorbell and the door opened; a small woman with silver gray hair answered; 'do come in

Detective Sergeant,' she led the way down a short passage into a high ceilinged room at the rear of the house.

The furniture was old, but well cared for and the place was immaculate; there was an aspidistra in a large brass container near the window and the only token of modernity was a small black and white television in a corner of the room. There was a fire burning cheerily in the cast iron fireplace and Miss Bird ushered him in and bade him be seated.

'Would you care for a cup of tea?' she inquired, 'I generally make myself one at this time!'

Cooper thanked her and she excused herself and went out of the room; he looked around for pictures of family, but there were none to be seen; he supposed that being a Miss and in Service most of her life she had not acquired a family and her relatives had all passed away. She returned shortly bearing a tray with a teapot, sugar bowl, milk jug and two large cups and saucers.

Setting them on the table she said; 'how do you like your tea? er I find your title rather long, would you think it impertinent of me if I called you Mr. Cooper?'

'Of course not Miss Bird and I take my tea black with one sugar.'

As they drank their tea he asked her for her opinion of the Farringdon Wells family and her relationship with James.

She had an excellent memory and was clear in her opinions; 'I joined the family five years before Master James was sent to Boarding School.'

'He didn't come home very often as his father had a busy practice and many clients to represent.'

'His mother was a very quiet lady, rather withdrawn in fact and she seemed to be of a nervous disposition.'

'What made you think that?' interjected Cooper.

'Well, she was always more agitated when Mr.Farringdon Wells was at home; he was rather a stern sort of man and didn't like to be crossed.'

'What was his attitude towards his son?' asked Cooper.

'I don't think he cared much for him; he seemed to prefer the boy to permanently board at the school; I felt very sorry as he was quite a sensitive child and he always seemed lost on the few occasions that he came home.'

'He was very upset when his mother died, but as soon as the funeral was over his father sent him back to school; which seemed rather cruel to me.'

'Were you surprised when James joined the Army?' remarked Cooper.

'Why no, I think that there was nothing for him at home once his mother had passed away; the Army would at least give him a home of sorts.'

'Have you any idea why someone should want to kill him Miss Bird?' said Cooper.

She thought for a while and said; 'it must have been someone he knew in the Army that had some sort of grudge against him, that's the only reason I can think of.'

Cooper stood up: 'thank you Miss Bird you have been most helpful and it was a lovely cup of tea.'

'Oh, have you got to go already?' she said rising; 'I only wish I could be more helpful; but I'm sure you will catch whoever did it.'

She went with him to the door and watched him drive away.

Cooper was beginning to get a clearer picture of the character of James, Sebastian Farrington Wells.

CHAPTER SIX

The report from Forensics was on his desk when he arrived back at Bethel Street. The bullet was from a 38. Revolver; probably a Webley or a Smith and Wesson, both guns had been used during the Second World War. There were no fingerprints, the perpetrator had most likely worn gloves; neither were there any fibres on the Colonel's clothes that were not his. Cooper snorted disgustedly; the report was of little help in tracing whoever carried out this murder. He would have to contact the War Office and obtain details of personnel who served with Farrington Wells in the Western Desert. He rang Directory Enquiries and got the number in Whitehall; after being shunted around several departments he finally got Records and a bright lady answered.

'Hello; how may I help you?' an attractive voice asked. Cooper explained and she asked him which particular period of the Desert Campaign he required. He made an inspired guess at roughly the period during the Colonels capture and escape from the P.O.W camp. She said she would look up the information and ring him back. There was of course one other avenue of exploration and that was the Palace of Westminster. Surely there must be people there that knew him well and maybe could throw some light on this enigmatic person? It came through in the book that outside of the public persona little was really known of the Colonel's private life. There was no record of him being married or having any offspring, in fact his private life was a closed book. He left a message at Westminster requesting a list of names of MPs who knew the Colonel, explaining the urgency of the murder inquiry. Well he had cast his bread upon the waters and would have to wait and see what returned on the next tide.

CHAPTER SEVEN

At three that afternoon Foley answered a call and handed the phone to Cooper; the caller identified himself as Michael Swift, Farrington Wells's secretary.

'Hello Detective Sergeant, I have just received your enquiry and will make myself available for questioning if you think it will help you.'

Cooper thanked him and arranged a meeting for the following morning; putting down the phone he remarked to Foley;

'I don't suppose he will be able to throw much light on who could have killed his boss; but he may know something about his War record that the guy who wrote the biography has missed.'

'Perhaps he can point you towards some of his constituents who knew him during the war; suggested Foley.'

'Good thinking Foley, that is definitely an avenue to follow up; we'll make a detective out of you yet my lad.'

The lad pulled a face; 'anything that gets me out of the office Guv is welcome, when I joined the police I had no idea how much of my time would be taken up by paper work.'

'It's all part of being a policeman Foley; which reminds me; how are this year's Records of detection going?'

The lad groaned; 'That's not fair Guv, a veritable blow below the belt; I should have them completed by Friday.

Cooper grinned; 'well see that you do, because 'Paper Clips' will want them on his desk first thing; otherwise we will be in the proverbial.'

The next morning he arrived at the House of Commons and was shown up to Michael Swift's office. It was remarkably small and gloomy; the secretary on the other hand was an energetic young man immaculately dressed in a pinstriped suit, patent leather shoes and a rather flamboyant tie. He greeted Cooper warmly, shaking his hand and waving him towards a chair next to a coat stand.

'Have you been to Westminster before Detective Sergeant?' he asked; as Cooper started to reply a young woman with horn rimmed glasses entered the room bearing a tray.

'Put it over there Daphne there's a dear;' said Swift; turning to Cooper he said; 'do you like your coffee black without or milk and sugar?'

'Black without,' mumbled Cooper, rather overwhelmed by Swift's rapid rate of conversation.

Daphne completed her ministrations and left the room; sipping his coffee then realising that it was far too hot, Cooper set it down again.

Swift leant back in his chair and placed his hands together as if in prayer; 'now I have no idea how I can help you, but fire away and we shall see how it goes.'

'I'm trying to get information which will help me to find likely lines of inquiry Mr. Swift....

'Please do call me Michael; there's no need to be so formal.' Swift interjected.

'As I was saying er Michael there is very little to go on at this time; the forensic evidence is unhelpful and I need to gather a group of possible suspects in order to progress.'

'Well I must say I don't see where I can be of much help to you; my relationship with Colonel Farrington Wells was mainly of a professional nature; but perhaps I can put you in touch with some of the members who may be able to enlighten you as to his contacts.'

'As you may have deduced he was a very private individual, despite his many good works.'

'Yes I had got that impression;" said Cooper wearily.

Swift looked at his watch; standing up he said, 'If you would like to follow me I will take you through to where the MPs meet their constituents, there are a couple of likely candidates for you to talk to.'

He went off at a cracking pace with Cooper trying to keep up; Swift by name and by nature, thought Cooper. They went down the corridor then down a flight of stairs eventually coming out on to a large terrace overlooking the Thames. There were several groups of people seeking advice from their MPs as Swift threaded his way through the throng.

He stopped at one of the tables where a large bearded man was in conversation with several people. He touched the man on the arm and whispered something in his ear; a frown flitted over the man's face, then he excused himself and stood up.

Coming over he extended his large hand and Cooper was treated to one of the strongest hand shakes he had ever experienced.

'This is Sir Richard Coombs, member for Haveford West, Detective Sergeant: he was in the Long Range Desert Group with the late Colonel Farrington Wells;' said Swift.

'You will have to excuse me as there is a lot of clearing up to do before the Colonel's successor arrives; don't hesitate to get in touch if you require any more assistance;' with that he was gone leaving Cooper and Sir Richard regarding one another speculatively.

'What exactly is it you want to know?' asked the MP.

Cooper explained that he was trying to establish a motive for the murder of Farrington Wells.

'Do you fancy a drink Inspector?'
Cooper gave a wry smile; 'I'm afraid I'm only a lowly
Detective Sergeant Sir Richard, but I could certainly go a
pint of bitter.'
'Splendid; and I'll have a G&T; just go to the bar and tell
Manning I sent you.'
Cooper decided that he had been had; this man needed
watching.

He did as he was bid and ordered the drinks; when he
attempted to pay the barman waved him away; 'no sir
these go onto Sir Richard's account.'
He set the drinks down on the table and slipped into the chair
opposite the MP;
Coombs raised his glass and said; 'to a successful
conclusion of your quest.'
Cooper sipped his bitter speculatively while he decided on his
approach; this man would be difficult to interrogate as he was
used to playing with words.
'What was your impression of Sir Farrington Wells when
you were together in the Desert Campaign?'
Coombs grimaced and said; 'He would have made a
damned good Poker player; inscrutable and very self
contained.'
'Didn't he mix with the other officers?' asked Cooper.
'When it was necessary, like Dining in Nights and
concert parties; that sort of thing, but he was considered
a loner by most of the chaps,' responded Sir Richard.
'What about his attitude in combat situations; there was
no hint of lack of moral fibre?'
'Good Lord no, he was always in the forefront of any
action; no nothing wrong there.'
'Was he ever married?' asked Cooper speculatively.

'Not that I ever heard of,' responded Coombs, 'he seemed to be thoroughly bound up in his career, one of these self fulfilled characters I suppose.'

Cooper began to realise that he was unlikely to glean any further information from this man; either he was unwilling to elaborate on what he knew about Farrington Wells or his ignorance was genuine. He drank the remainder of his bitter and stood up; enduring that vice like handshake again he thanked Coombs for his time and headed for the exit.

CHAPTER EIGHT

Foley was waiting for him as he reached the door of his office; 'I've had a phone call from the lady at the War Office Guv; apparently Farrington Whatnot was a member of a Club in Portland Street.'
Cooper pricked up his ears; 'What's it called Foley?'
'I've got it written down here Guv' said Foley; adding rather shamefacedly, 'I had to get her to spell it.'
Cooper glanced at the paper and smiled; 'it's called the Misogynist Club.'
'What's that when it's up and dressed Guv?'
'A Misogynist is someone who doesn't like women Foley.'
'What you mean someone who's gay?'
'Not necessarily; very often they are people who don't wish to have the responsibility of a wife and children.'
'I must say that I'm surprised that Farrington Wells was a member of any Club; that rather presupposes that he was a gregarious soul, which he certainly wasn't by all account.'
'Anyhow it will have to be followed up; God knows we have little enough to go on at the moment.'
He rang the Club and made an appointment to speak to the secretary, a certain Caractacus Pym. He took a taxi from Liverpool Street to the Club; paying off the driver he looked up at the Georgian façade resplendent with Doric pillars and Shell portico, the place oozed privilege before he had even crossed the threshold. His feet sank into the pile of the carpet as he approached the reception desk where an ancient retainer

greeted him with a certain amount of deference. He stated his business and the old fellow led him into the inner sanctum saying that the secretary was expecting him and would be with him in a few minutes. Cooper had barely settled into a leather arm chair before a rotund bespectacled man with an egg shaped head completely devoid of hair and dressed in dog toothed pattern trousers and a cut away coat ambled into the room. He looked myopically over the rims of his half lens glasses at Cooper with the expression of someone who had just discovered a new life form.

'Good Day er Inspector Cooper; to what do I owe this visitation from the Arm of the Law?'

Cooper stood up and extended his hand which was duly inspected with care before it was shaken with a cold limp response.

Cooper experienced a spasm of revulsion; however he summoned a smile and said 'I'm afraid that I am only a Detective Sergeant Mr.Pym, but thanks for the promotion.'

There was not even a flicker of amusement from the man who significantly glanced at his watch.

'I hope this matter won't take long Sergeant; the annual accounts are being presented this week and I have to ensure that they are available for scrutiny by the Chairman.'

Cooper said; 'As you are no doubt aware Mr. Pym one of your members has been murdered and I am trying to find a motive which will ultimately bring the killer to justice.'

'Can you give me any information that would help me to apprehend that person?'

I am aware of the demise of Sir James, but I'm afraid there is nothing outside of the running of the Club that I can help you with; the rules are that a member's private life is strictly his own;' the man stated.

'Was there anyone here that had a grudge against him or disliked him sufficiently to wish him harm?' Cooper persisted

'I haven't the faintest idea Sergeant; I rarely met Sir James on a social level, only being involved in the administration of the organisation.'

Cooper was beginning to lose his patience with this stuffed shirt.

'Surely you must have an idea of the relationships formed in a place of this status, this is where the Great and the Good relax and I doubt that even you would be unaware of differences of opinion and even quarrels especially at this level?'

The man's jaw dropped; recovering somewhat he spluttered; 'how dare you speak to me like that; I would have you know that I have faithfully served this Institution for twenty three years without a word of reproach; I shall be contacting your superior to lodge an official complaint.'

'Perhaps you would like to come with me to do that;' said Cooper; 'and I will have great pleasure in charging you with obstructing the police in carrying out their duty.'

The man visibly wilted as Cooper went on; 'for whatever reason you have deliberately set out to obstruct my enquiries; your indifference might do you credit in certain circumstances; but this is a murder enquiry and it is your duty to assist the police in any way you can.'

Pym was deflated like a pricked balloon; 'Perhaps I was a bit hasty Sergeant; but things have been rather hectic recently and I am under considerable stress….

.Cooper cut across his attempt to justify his attitude.

'Now I'm prepared to overlook your previous reticence providing you tell me what you know about Sir James and his acquaintances.'

'Certainly Sergeant; I shall be only too pleased to help in any way I can.'

Cooper had utter contempt for this pompous 'Jobs worth'; however he knew in his heart of hearts that he wouldn't get much out of him

This proved to be the case and after a further series of question revealed that in fact Pym knew very little about the members Cooper gave up and caught the next train back to Norwich.

CHAPTER NINE

Foley was waiting as he came into the office and launched into an excited report.

'There's been a break in at the house of Farrington Wells Guv.'

Cooper stopped in his tracks; 'what have forensics found?'

'Don't know Guv, they are still there; the sergeant in charge rang and asked for you.'

When he arrived at the scene it was a hive of activity; as well as Forensic there were several Constables busy making house to house enquiries. He ducked under the Crime Scene tape and entered the house; finding the Duty Sergeant he asked what if anything had been taken.

The man looked puzzled; 'that's the odd thing, nothing of any worth seems to be missing, even though there were plenty of antiques; pictures and items of value.'

'What about documents, letters etc?"

'No, not that we can see;' responded the sergeant.

'Is there a wall safe here?' asked Cooper.

'Yes in the study behind the picture;' said the man.

Cooper went into the study and lifted an oil painting of a seascape which revealed an expensive looking circular safe behind. On looking closely he noticed that there were scratches around the keyhole as if someone had been trying to open it.

He called through to the Sergeant; 'do we have the key to this thing?'

The sergeant joined him and said 'No we looked through all the drawers and on the desk, but no joy I'm afraid Dan.'

Cooper grunted and went over to the roll top bureau which proved to be locked; he picked up a steel letter opener from the desk and inserted it at the bottom of the roll top. Giving it a quick twist he was rewarded by a loud cracking sound and the top rolled up to reveal the inside of the bureau.

Turning to the sergeant he said; 'that was lucky it was open all the time.'

He carefully searched every cubbyhole finding several keys, none of which fitted the wall safe.

Damn! Where the hell could it be? he thought.

There was a scarcely noticeable break in the edge of the desk; he felt under it and pressed a small protrusion; a slim drawer shot out; obviously a secret hideaway. There nestling on the green baize was a key; Cooper picked it up and walked across to the wall safe.

Sure enough it fitted and he opened the safe; 'Bingo.' he said triumphantly.

Inside were several documents, a case containing various valuables and a bundle of letters tied with red tape.

CHAPTER TEN

Cooper removed the contents from the safe and deposited them on the table. He sifted through the documents, most of which were deeds of various kinds, but one particular document attracted his attention. At the top of the first page was a heraldic symbol in the shape of an eagle with outstretched wings holding the world in its talons; what made his heart skip a beat was the swastika emblazoned on the globe.

'What the…?'

It was all in German and began 'Sei gerte mine herr;' he understood that bit, but the rest would have to be interpreted.

His mind reeled at the implications of this letter; what was a British MP doing communicating with a Nazi organisation?

He scooped up the documents and had them bagged and numbered; then he took them back to the station. Cooper made a phone call to the University of East Anglia Language Department and asked for a German speaker. A guttural voice answered and Cooper found himself talking to a certain Herr Faulkus. He explained the reason for the call and asked if he could have the document translated.

'It vould be a pleasure Sergeant; I could come over dis afternoon if you vish.'

Faulkus arrived promptly and was ushered into an interview room; Cooper brought the document down and after ordering two coffees he laid the papers in front of the interpreter.

Faulkus donned a pair of thick lens glasses and peered at the

Logo.

He looked up at Cooper and said; 'vere did you get zis document?'

'I'm sorry; said Cooper; but I am not at liberty to say at the moment and I would stress that this is not to be mentioned outside this room as its evidence in an ongoing case.'

'I understand; said Faulkus; "but I must inform you dat dis document iss from der APWEHR dated 12 October 1941 to von of its agents.'

He went on; 'it iss instructions for zer agent to send information regarding de disposition of der British Army in de desert.'

Light was beginning to dawn in Coopers mind; Farrington Wells had been a spy. No wonder he had been killed; the problem now was that the range of suspects could include the Security organisations; this could become very tricky indeed, both from a Security and a Political point of view. Cooper realised that he would have to move very carefully from now on. It was time to consult his superiors; he thanked Herr Faulkus and escorted him to the door. Back in the office he picked up the phone and rang for an appointment with Trafford. Chief Superintendent Trafford had always had a soft spot for Cooper, much to Inspector Grant's chagrin. He admired the man's dogged determination; his initiative and most of all his refusal to be overawed by authority. He listened carefully as the Sergeant outlined the facts relating to the documents found in Farrington Wells's safe and the implications that they raised.

'My God you've certainly opened a tricky can of worms Cooper;' Trafford remarked, 'what do you want me to do?'

'Well sir I was hoping that you would contact MI5 and ask if they have a file on this case.'

'That's the very least of it Cooper; I think MI6 need to be consulted as well in view of what has happened to Farrington Wells; this may well be a political killing of some kind and if so they will take over the investigation.' 'Leave it with me Cooper and I will contact the Home Office to discuss a way forward in this case.'

'In the meantime carry on with the investigation until you hear from me.'
Cooper left the 'Super's' office in a thoughtful mood; When this business got into the public domain the 'whatsit' was really going to hit the fan. Also it probably meant that he would be taken off the case once it got into the hands of the Security Services. He resented the fact that having got this far he would have to hand every thing over to some civil servant.
As he entered his office Foley greeted him; 'Hullo Guv I've got some interesting information from these letters.'
He had been given the bundle from the safe to go through whilst Cooper had been with the Chief Superintendent.
'What revelations have you found Foley? said Cooper eagerly.
'It turns out that Farringtron Wells was in regular contact with an organisation in Argentina called the Teutonic Warriors Guv.' 'I've tried to find out any information on them, but so far I've drawn a blank.'
'Sounds like some sort of Nazi revival group Foley; plenty of their elite fled to South America towards the end of the War.'
'Bit before my time Guv; what do they hope to achieve now that Hitler is dead and Germany's been divided up?'
Probably plotting a resurgence of Nazi-ism Foley; heaven help us all if they succeed.' 'The pressing question is how did Farrington Wells fit into all this; have you read all the letters?' Cooper asked.

'I'm about half way through Guv.'

Cooper sat down at his desk; 'give me half of the unread ones and we had better go through them to see if there are any further clues as to what they're up to.'

CHAPTER ELEVEN

Günther Löeb gazed absently down onto the factory floor through the office window. His mind was elsewhere as he had just received the news of Farrington Wells's murder. This development had serious implications for the future plans of the Teutonic Warriors. Farrington Wells had been a source of great influence for them in the UK and would be difficult to replace. He turned and walked back to his desk; picking up the phone he asked for a line and dialed the Chairman of the organisation.

A cultured voice answered in Spanish; Löeb cut across it saying; 'We had best converse in English Herr Von Richter.'

'Very well Günther; what is it that you wish to discuss?'

Löeb outlined the events of the murder and there was a long silence at the other end of the line.

Finally Von Richter said slowly; 'this alters our plans considerably, the man was the key to the British end of the programme.'

'I think we will have to call a meeting and send an emissary to England to contact a replacement.'

'Perhaps you will organise that at once Günter?'

Yawole mine Herr, it shall be done; I will advise you of the meeting date when arranged.'

He clicked his heels and replaced the phone before striding out of the room. 'As he went down in the lift Loeb felt elated; it was good to be working for the Cause.' Just like old times when he was in the Waffen SS and Von Richter was his

General. Memories of their campaigns on the Russian Front when Germany was in the ascendancy came flooding back; how they had brushed aside those Communist blockheads in their lightning advance. Then Stalingrad and the shameful surrender; the long march to the Goolags in Siberia; his escape together with his General and the privations during their long journey back to the Fatherland. Seeing the devastation they had been fortunate to escape to Argentina through the Odessa organisation which helped many Nazis to start a new life in South AmericaHe had been lucky as he got the funding to build a factory producing accessories for the aircraft industries in the USA and business was booming.

He walked out of the building to his Mercedes soft top and set off for his home.

CHAPTER TWELVE

Cooper finished reading the last of the letters from Farrington Wells's safe and sat back; his mind in a turmoil.
This man was not only a spy for the Nazi 'ex-pats,' but they were planning something that was going to be a threat to the Western World; but what? That was the million dollar question; there were vague references in the letters, but nothing which would give him a clue as to what it might be.

The phone rang and Foley answered it; putting his hand over the mouthpiece he called, 'It's for you Guv.'

It was Trafford; 'Hallo Cooper; I've been instructed by the Home Secretary to continue the inquiry into the murder of Sir James; however the Security Services will be conducting their own investigations into the matters that have arisen since the break in at his home.'

Cooper was relieved; 'Thank you sir, that's great news; incidentally I have some letters which tie him into a German organisation in Argentina which will be of interest to the 'spooks.'

'Oh really Cooper? Perhaps you will send them up to me and I will pass them on.'

Cooper did a wry grin; 'nosey old bugger', he thought.

'Very good sir I'll send Foley up with them straight away.'

He rang off and collecting the letters which he put back in the evidence bag and sent Foley off to deliver them.

There had been considerable speculation by the Media regarding the break in and Cooper had fended them off so far;

but he knew that sooner or later a statement would have to be made as to the progress or otherwise of the case, especially of a Public Figure of such stature as Farrington Wells If the whole truth came into the Public domain there would be a scandal of gigantic proportions, the ramifications of which would reverberate around the world There was much more to this case than plain old fashioned murder and Cooper could see that it was already widening into an International conspiracy. He had to follow this aspect of the case to find the reason for and who was responsible for the killing, but how?

CHAPTER THIRTEEN

The meeting had been convened and by a show of hands
Günther had been appointed representative of the Teutonic
Warriors in England. As he sat in the reception area of
Buenos Aires Airport he was glowing with pride at the
thought that he should have been trusted with such an
important mission. His baggage was already checked in and
he was waiting for the announcement to move into the
embarkation area. Eventually the message came; 'passengers
for the Frankfurt flight please assemble at Gate 9.' He picked
up his overnight bag and made for the elevator; he was so
intent on getting the plane that he failed to notice an
inconspicuous man in a scruffy raincoat following him. David
Schoenberg had been keeping him under observation for
several months now. Mossad had picked him for this task
since they started taking an interest in this Nazi organisation.
They had been active in Argentina since the end of the war
and had already managed to kidnap several high ranking War
Criminals and smuggle them to Israel for trial. However this
was a shadowing operation in order to find out just what these
guys were up to. They boarded the plane and soon the engines
whined into life and the tractor backed the airliner out of the
parking bay. She trundled round the perimeter track onto the
end of the runway; the pilot ran up the engines to full power,
released the brakes and she quickly gathered speed down the
rain soaked tarmac. Rotating on reaching take off speed it
climbed off the runway into the louwering cloud cover;
Günther was on his way. He slept most of the way across the

Atlantic, eventually being awoken by the announcement that they would be landing at Frankfurt in two hours. On disembarking he cleared Customs and went into the men's toilets to freshen up. As he looked in the mirror he caught the eye of a man loitering around the cubicles; the man immediately looked away and began using the hand dryer. Günther completed his ablutions, picked up his bag and went out; later he spotted the same man hovering on the fringe of the crowd; he was being tailed. He went into the Concourse and looked at the arrival board; the London plane had arrived and was due out in one hour. Then he went over to the News Stand and purchased a paper; casually looking around he spotted the man standing near the exit. Günther decided to string along with the situation until he reached London, then if the guy was still tailing him he would decide what to do.

CHAPTER FOURTEEN

The phone was ringing as Cooper reached his office; picking it up he found it was Michael Swift, Farrington Well's secretary.

'Oh hello Detective Sergeant; I have an apology to make.'

'Really?' said Cooper wondering what this confession was about.

'Yes I realised after I left you last week that I had promised to introduce you to all the people that knew Sir James from way back.' He continued; 'the other person I had intended you to meet was not in the House at the time, but he is available now if you wish to interview him.'

'Who would that be?' said Cooper.

'Oh; forgive me.' said Swift, 'I meant to say Bernard Fisher, MP for Huddersfield.'

'When can I meet him?' asked Cooper.

'Well, tomorrow morning he is meeting some of his constituents and I mentioned you were conducting enquiries into Sir James's death; he was quite keen to meet you.'

'll be there Michael, thank you for letting me know; look forward to seeing you again;' Cooper rang off as Foley came into the office.

'I shall be in London tomorrow Foley, hold the fort and log any messages for me.'

'Right Guv;' Foley replied as he set down two mugs of coffee, 'PC Brett is setting a new record for fried breakfasts this morning.'

'I'm surprised he has the time to go on the beat;' said Cooper; 'he seems to spend most of his time in the canteen.'

'Probably compensation for a barren love life;' observed Foley.

'Enough of this badinage Foley; time to earn your corn; anyhow you're not supposed to know about such things at your age.'

Foley assumed his best hard done by expression and began going through the files on his desk.

The phone rang again and Foley answered; turning to Cooper he said; 'it's for you Guv.'

Taking the phone Cooper asked who was speaking; 'This is Tony Hart from Section 3 Security, Sergeant.'

CHAPTER FIFTEEN

What can I do for you Mr. Hart;" said Cooper?
'It's what I am doing for you Detective Sergeant; call it a Quid pro Quo in return for the letters you sent us; they were most helpful.'
'I'm sending round a file for your eyes only; the Courier should be there by lunch time; Bye now,' with that he rang off.
Mystified, Cooper put down the phone; what on earth was going on? MI5 were not renowned for their co-operation with Plod; he sipped his coffee, it was cold.
He got to the House just as Big Ben was striking ten o clock; booked in and was shown up to Swift's office
The secretary jumped up and shook his hand; 'nice to see you again Dan, I've made an appointment with Bernard for ten thirty if that's OK with you; would you like a coffee for you while you are waiting?'
Cooper affirmed and sat down; 'how's it going with your new boss?' he enquired.
Michael laughed; 'he hasn't arrived yet; the by-election takes place next week.'
'Who's the candidate?'
'A local land owner called Cargill; a safe pair of hands, he's been associated with the local branch for years.'
The coffee arrived as they were chatting and shortly after Swift glanced at his watch; 'we may as well get going to the West Wing and I'll introduce you to Bernard Fisher.'
They seemed to spend an inordinate amount of time traveling through numerous corridors before arriving outside an office door with the MP's name on.

Swift knocked and opened the door beckoning Cooper inside; 'Good morning Minister; May I introduce Detective Sergeant Cooper.'

Cooper shook hands whilst surveying the man in front of him; he was thin and had a slight stoop, nevertheless there was something commanding about his demeanor and his hand shake was firm.

'A pleasure to meet you Sergeant.' he said; the smile was friendly, but the eyes belied the smile; they were guarded and searching as if he were trying to ascertain Cooper's motivation. 'How may I be of service to you?' the voice, although cultured had a trace of North Country about it, Cooper guessed Tyneside or Durham.

Cooper explained what he was hoping to find out about the demise of Sir James.

Fisher waved him into a chair and sat down behind his desk; 'what do you want to know about him; his War Record? That speaks for itself; they don't hand out Military Cross's like sweets.'

'I'm trying to find a motive for his death;' replied Cooper; 'everyone that I've spoken to already seemed to know very little about the man himself.'

'That's because he didn't want people to get close to him; he was a very self contained person;' responded Fisher; 'he was definitely not one of the herd.'

'How did you come to meet him Minister?' asked Cooper.

'In the desert, after he had escaped from the German POW camp at Biserta.'

'I had been seconded to the Long Range Desert Group which was just being formed and I subsequently worked with him on several missions behind enemy lines.'

'He was absolutely fearless and the sort you could rely on in a tight spot; he got us out of several extremely 'hairy' situations; it was as though he bore a charmed life.'

Cooper thought to himself; if only you knew the truth; that the man was a German spy.

'Was there anything odd about him that you could remember; or anyone that he didn't get on with?'

Fisher considered for a moment then said; 'he would sometimes go off into the desert on his own for hours, eventually returning looking fatigued.'

'We put it down to some sort of release from the strain of combat; it took some people like that,' mused Fisher.

'More likely to commune with his Nazi masters.' thought Cooper.

Fisher looked at his watch; standing up he said; 'I'm afraid I will have to leave you as my constituents are waiting ; I hope that I've been of some help Detective Sergeant God knows, I would have liked to help you more, but he was pretty inscrutable; renowned for it in fact.' They shook hands and Fisher asked his secretary to escort Cooper to the main doors.

CHAPTER SIXTEEN

As they went down the corridor from Fisher's office Cooper saw a large florid faced man coming towards them; there was something familiar about him; he had seen this man somewhere before, but where. He turned in time to see the man entering Fisher's office; it was only in the taxi taking him back to Liverpool Street station that he remembered; it was the man in the photograph that had been sent in the file from MI5. What was a representative of the Teutonic Warriors doing contacting a British MP? On returning to Bethel Street he picked up the phone and obtained a line to MI5 Headquarters, asking for Tony Hart.

'Hallo Detective Sergeant; did you receive the file?'

'That's what I'm ringing about;' said Cooper and went on to describe his sighting of Löeb at Westminster.

'Well done;' said Hart excitedly;'so the man has arrived in England; I'll put a tail on him straight away.'

'The question is; what is his connection to Fisher?' said Cooper.

'The man is well known for his extreme Right Wing views;' replied Hart, 'he was a friend of Mosely before the War and attended his rallies.' 'There is definitely some scheme being hatched by this group in Argentina which involves well placed persons in our Government and we had better get to the bottom of it quickly.'

'This all begins to make sense now that we know that Farrington Wells worked for the Germans during the war and was involved with these people before he was murdered.' Cooper said. 'They are probably looking for a replacement; that's why Löeb has been sent over here.' he continued.

'Yes, that makes sense;' replied Hart; 'point is, we have to find out exactly what they're up to, which means keeping both men under surveillance; we shall obviously monitor all Fisher's calls, although I doubt that we shall glean much information from them; he will be on his guard now.'

'More likely they will communicate by meets in some location which can't be bugged; like a park or some other open space.' 'Keep up the good work at your end;' said Hart breezily and I'll notify you of any development that affects you; Bye for now.'

With that he rang off leaving Cooper with a mind full of questions.

CHAPTER SEVENTEEN

Günther emerged from Westminster feeling pleased with the interview he had had with Bernard Fisher; it was obvious that they were two like minded people. He had outlined the plans that were being proposed by the Teutonic Warriors to a receptive audience it seemed and Fisher had eagerly plied him with questions. Gunther had arranged a further meeting in a few days time, but not at 'The House'; that guy who had been tailing him was on the terrace all during their conversation; he would have to do something about that one. On returning to his hotel he went up to his room, bathed and changed for dinner, after a couple of drinks in the bar he went outside; sure enough the man in the raincoat was hovering just down the street. Günter crossed the road and walked a short distance before ducking into an alley which backed onto a restaurant. He noticed that there were two of the large industrial bins that food outlets used standing outside the door. He quickly slipped behind them and waited; sure enough he heard the pattering of feet as his tail hurried to catch him up. Just as the man passed the bins Günther caught him by the throat and dragged him behind the bins. His muscular hands quickly dispatched the luckless individual and he opened the lid of the nearest bin and stuffed the lifeless body inside. Emerging from the alley he retraced his steps back to the hotel, had a couple of beers before going to bed, dropping into a dreamless sleep.

Next morning Cooper's phone was ringing as he arrived;

where was Foley he thought irritably.

He picked up and recognised Tony's voice at the other end, he sounded exited.

'Hallo Dan; all hell has broken out we've had a call from the Israeli Embassy regarding a murder near Southampton Row last night.'

'Who's been killed?' asked Cooper.

'Some Mossad agent; but here's the rub, not only was the guy here without notifying us what he was up to, but the Consul let slip he was tailing our mutual friend.'

'What, Löeb?' exclaimed Cooper incredulously?

'Just so;' responded Hart; 'this has really put the cat amongst the pigeons Dan; we know who's done it; but if he's arrested bang goes our chances of finding out what he's up to.'

Cooper was silent for a few moments; 'was your man in the vicinity at the time?'

'No he had gone back to the Section when Löeb went back to his hotel after meeting with the Minister.'

Cooper said; 'pity, he could have been a witness for when Löeb is arrested.'

Hart agreed; 'Yes, but look on the bright side; we've still got him under surveillance and he thinks he's got away with it.'

'I'm afraid that doesn't help me with my enquiries;' said Cooper sadly.

CHAPTER EIGHTEEN

Von Richter parked his BMW outside the main building of the Murkel Pharmaceutical Company and entered the impressive foyer; the centrepiece of which was a large fountain spouting ever changing coloured water. He walked up to reception and introduced himself to a good looking girl behind the counter.

'Welcome Herr Von Richter; Doktor Murkel is expecting you; I will show you to his office.' She led the way up a flight of stairs to a suite of glass cubicles containing offices and small laboratories.

The girl knocked respectfully at the last door in the corridor and a muffled voice called; 'Commen Sie.

'Herr Von Richter is here Herr Doktor;'

'Ah Wilcommen Herr Von Richter he cried, waving towards a chair; 'sitzen sie bitte.'

They exchanged pleasantries for a while; continuing to speak German; eventually Von Richter said; 'To business Herr Doktor; you have something to show me?'

'Yawol Excellency, I have it here.' he pulled open a drawer in his desk and brought out a small clear plastic box containing half a dozen phials containing a greenish liquid; pushing it across the desk he smiled, 'there is enough in this little box to wipe out a large city.'

'We are not envisaging just one city Doktor; this is the weapon that will enable us to turn the dreams of our Fuhrer into reality.' Von Richter said reprovingly.

'We now have sufficient stocks of Mn43 to wipe out the entire population of the world,' crowed Merkel, beside himself with glee.

Von Richter looked contemptuously at him; the man was a scientific genius, but he was like many of his kind, unstable.

'Have the tests been fully successful?' asked Von Richter.

'Oh, yes Excellency, would you like me to arrange a demonstration for you; it would not take long to organise it?'

Von Richter looked purposefully at his watch; 'no thank you Doctor, I'm sure you know what you are doing; you will see that a sample is sent to Herr Löeb at this address;' he took a piece of paper from his breast pocket and laid it on the desk.

'Yawhol mine Herr; it will be a privilege to serve the Fatherland.' he insisted in accompanying Von Richter to his car still babbling continuously.

As he drove away; Von Richter thought; why do we have to rely on these inferior individuals to achieve our ambitions. Ultimately there will have to be a second cull to weed out the intellectuals; they spend too much time thinking rather than being like the Teutonic Warrior who gains his goal through action.

CHAPTER NINETEEN

In an office in a rather seedy part of downtown Buenos Airies Gabriel Walfisch lit another cigarette; he was worried. He had just received a communication from headquarters in Tel Aviv that agent David Schoenberg had been found dead in London. This would have serious repercussions with relations with Britain; not only was David working undercover, but there had been no interchange of information with MI5.

There would be questions in the House of Commons and the Tabloid Press would have a field day with it. The last thing Mossad needed was this unwelcome publicity and it would make the surveillance of Löeb virtually impossible.

The British Secret Service would not be in the mood to co-operate; especially in view of the fact that they had not been informed of David's presence or his mission. He shrugged fatalistically and picked up the phone.

Cooper was explaining to Grant why he was not going to arrest Löeb and the Inspector was not impressed.

'It seems to me Cooper that this whole case is going nowhere at present and I don't mind telling you that I am under great pressure from our Political Masters to clear it up.'   '

'I can't arrest him until we know what he's up to sir; in any case I am having to work in conjunction with Security and they are certainly against moving in on Löeb until we have the complete picture.'

'These Nazi's have a definite agenda to recruit certain influential figures in this country and until we know the why and the wherefore our hands are tied.'

'You don't seem to be any further with finding who killed Sir James either Cooper.' retorted Grant.

'That's not fair sir; there is just not anything to go on at present; I'm sure evidence will be found as this case proceeds that will tie in with both murders.'

'Well, I hope for your sake that something turns up soon;' said Grant dryly; 'I don't know how long I can keep you on the case Cooper; our Masters are far from happy.'.

'Keep me informed daily Cooper and for God's sake make some progress.' Grant picked up a file on his desk and said; 'Close the door on your way out will you.'

CHAPTER TWENTY

Fisher had arranged to meet Löeb in Regents Park; Hart had contacted Cooper and they met in Maltlake High Street.

'I've deployed several people around the park:' said Hart, 'we should be able to get someone near enough to overhear their conversation.'

'Isn't that a bit risky,'"said Cooper; what if they're spotted?'

Hart laughed; "not with the listening devices we use; the agent can be thirty yards away walking the dog and can hear every word.'

They entered one of the gateways into the park and Hart thrust a bag of hazel nuts into Cooper's hand.

'This is in case we come on them unexpectedly; we find the nearest trees and feed the Red Squirrels.'

Cooper couldn't help a chuckle; 'is this a regular MI5 ploy?' he asked.

'Only in dire emergencies,' said Hart with a grin.

They made their way past the start of the Golf Course and on by the side of Beverley Brook. There seemed to be no sign of Fisher or Löeb at the moment, then Cooper spotted the couple in earnest conversation on the other side of the lake in the centre of the park. There was an elderly man with a Red Setter strolling along the footpath adjacent to the lake, seemingly deep in thought.

'Is that one of your men?' asked Cooper.

Before Hart could reply Löeb took Fisher by the arm and hurried away from the lake to the other side of the park.

'Damn;' said Hart; 'our man's been rumbled.'

'What happens now?' asked Cooper.

'It's OK. We've got plenty of people spread about the park who can take over;' Hart said.

They walked on till they came to the Park's refreshment kiosk; there were metal tables and chairs out front; Hart ordered a pot of tea and sat down at a table where he could keep an eye on developments. Cooper joined him and the tea arrived; Hart poured out and asked Cooper if he took milk and sugar.

'Black, one sugar please;' said Cooper stretching his legs under the table.

This is certainly what you would call a civilised way of conducting surveillance;' he said.

'Don't knock it,' replied Hart; 'it's better than standing outside in a downpour on a cold night.'

'I think I might apply for a transfer, if these are usual conditions working for MI5;' said Cooper sipping his tea with relish.

By now Löeb and Fisher were on the move making their way towards the main exit.

'Time to call in the team;' said Hart; obviously they've either finished or they have abandoned the meeting. You may as well come down to the Section and listen to what's been recorded.' Cooper was quite flattered; it's not every day that a humble Detective Sergeant from 'the sticks' gets an invite to MI5. They walked back to the car park in Maltlake and Hart unlocked a black BMW coupe.

'Another perk of the job?' observed Cooper enviously.

Hart laughed: 'Woe betide you if you bent it; you would still be paying for it after you retired.'

CHAPTER TWENTY ONE

Gunther Löeb was furious; it had been obvious that British Security had agents all over Regents Park. Whenever they stopped to talk someone immediately moved into their vicinity. This had got Fisher badly worried about his position and he was obviously getting cold feet. As Gunther traveled back to his hotel in the taxi he decided that he would have to contact Von Richter and get further guidance as to how to proceed.

Meanwhile at Section Three Hart was holding a meeting at which various recordings were being played through; unfortunately there seemed nothing of an incriminating nature on them due to the constant disruption of conversation as the targets moved on.

'This is an unmitigated disaster;' Hart exclaimed; 'all we've got is a series of garbled pieces of dialogue.'

'Excuse Me.' said Cooper, 'but in the fourth extract I noticed Löeb mentioned a series of letters and numbers; could we just play it back?'

The agent rewound the tape and started the recording; 'There, just there; could you just run that past me again.' said Cooper excitedly.

Löeb's voice began again; 'once we have sufficient supplies of Mn43 we can commence…'

Hart commented; 'it sounds like some form of chemical formula; can't say it rings a bell.'

He wrote it down on a slip of paper and handed it to one of the agents; 'slip down to the lab Stuart and ask Gerald if he's ever heard of it there's a good chap.' The man exited and Hart turned to Cooper; 'well spotted old man, perhaps they are planning an attack with nerve gas or some other fiendish device; like those Japanese fellers who used SARON in the underground in Tokyo.'

Cooper disagreed; 'Surely that would take an awful lot of operatives to attack all the major cities in the UK?'

'See what you mean,' said Hart rubbing his chin 'seems like we are going to have to follow this up in Argentina.'

Just then Stuart returned and whispered in Hart's ear; He nodded several times and then said:

'Gerald has never heard of it, which means that it is something that must have been developed in an Argentinean Drug company employed by the Teutonic Warriors or whatever they call themselves.' He said to Cooper; 'thanks for your help; I think we can take advantage of the situation that Mossad find themselves in and lean on them to do the detective work in Argentina.'

'They are better equipped for it anyway; can I run you down to the station Dan?'

CHAPTER TWENTY TWO

Gabriel Walfisch replaced the phone; there were beads of sweat on his brow which were not caused by the weather.

He had just been ordered to co-operate with British Security by the Director of Mossad in Tel Aviv. They had told him in no uncertain terms that the shadowing mission he had organised had been badly bungled; not only had he lost a useful operative, but Mossad had been seriously compromised in what could have been a serious International incident.

He wiped his sweating brow and called through to his colleague Simon Kossof; 'can you come through Simon? I want to discuss something with you?'

Kossof was a slim unassuming fellow in his mid forties; he had an olive complexion, grey eyes and a handsome face.

He was a very experienced operative and had been involved in several abduction operations in South America.

'Yes Gabriel what is it you wish to discuss with me?' he said, slipping into the chair beside Walfisch's desk.

'It is about the Teutonic Warriors investigation;' Gabriel said grimly; 'it seems that it has gone badly wrong.' He repeated the gist of the phone call he had received and added; 'so you see we are in the unfortunate position of being forced to help the British in this matter.'

He went on to explain exactly what MI5 had requested.

Simon's eyes narrowed; 'I can't say I am overjoyed to help the British; my family was badly treated when they arrived in Israel after the war.'

Walfisch shrugged his shoulders hopelessly; 'I know; but what can I do?'

'We have no choice Gabriel; but it does not sit well with me to be co-erced into helping them.' 'What is it they want us to do Gabriel?'

'Track down and penetrate the source of a chemical weapon the Nazis are making;' replied Wofisch.

Simon leaned back in his chair and whistled softly; 'so they are on the rise again, do these Nazis ever give up?'

'Not until we have brought them all to justice,'replied Walfisch fiercely. 'It will not be easy; these people are ruthless and do not hesitate to kill, as we know by the loss of poor David.'

Simon stood up; 'leave it with me Gabriel, I shall start making enquiries straight away and report back.'

'For God's sake be careful Simon; I can't afford to lose you as well.'

Kossov smiled; 'I don't intend to allow those pigs to have that pleasure Gabriel; I will see you soon.' he turned and strode out of the room.

CHAPTER TWENTY THREE

Günther Löeb was apprehensive as he waited for his call to be put through to Buenos Aires. That Von Richter would be annoyed at the present situation was an understatement.
Apart from that he felt that he had failed to carry out his mission in converting Fisher to the cause. The familiar cultured voice of his leader interrupted his thoughts.
'Hello Günther, what have you to report?'
Löeb unhappily conveyed the situation to his leader.
'So, you are telling me that he has been frightened off by the attentions of British Security?' 'Who in all probability were alerted by your rash disposal of this Jewish agent? Gunther was unable to think of a suitable response; 'I thought it best to ring you at once Herr Oberst for further advice on how to proceed.'
There was an edge of menace in Von Richter's voice as he replied; 'This will require some further thought Günther; thanks to your bungling efforts it has set back the programme for the time being.' 'I think you had better come back as your cover is blown and no doubt the Authorities will have you under surveillance.' with that he rang off leaving Gunther feeling extremely vulnerable.
He packed his case, went down to reception and paid his bill; the receptionist said; 'leaving us Mr.Löeb?'I hope we see you again soon.' He muttered something unintelligible and went out to hail a taxi. The agent from Section Three folded his paper and started the engine of his Ford Escort; having spotted Löebe coming out of the

hotel and getting into a taxi. He followed it going in a Westerly direction as he phoned in to report.

'Hello George here; our target is on the move, looks as if he's heading for Heathrow.'

Hart came on the phone; 'keep with him George and we will alert Security at the airport to detain him; there is a Warrant out for him already.'

'OK sir will do.'

Sure enough the taxi cleared the centre of London and joined the Windsor road; Löeb was definitely trying to leave the country.

CHAPTER TWENTY FOUR

Günther paid off the taxi driver and made for the entrance of the Airport Booking hall. The next flight to Frankfurt left in two hours; he bought a ticket and walked over to the News Stand As he was selecting a paper he was suddenly aware of a burly individual ether side of him.

One laid his hand on his arm and said; 'would you come with us sir, there are some questions we would like to ask you?'

He looked wildly around for a means of escape; but the man who had spoken gripped his arm and said quietly; 'now sir we don't want to make a scene do we?'

Gunther felt the muzzle of a gun pressed into his side and decided that for now escape was out of the question.

'What am I being arrested for?' he blustered, 'I am a citizen of Argentina and my papers are all in order.'

'All in good time sir.' said the man soothingly; as they moved across the Entrance hall towards the glass doors.

Outside there was an unmarked car waiting and he was carefully put into the back seat with one man either side of him. The car pulled out into the traffic stream and headed back towards London. They arrived at Bow Street Police Station where he was arraigned and charged with murder.

Later sitting in a cell without his shoes and tie; he frantically reviewed his position; how had the police caught up with him so fast? Half an hour later he was taken into an interview room where a man dressed in a Saville Row suit, sporting a Lords yellow and red tie was sitting with another man in plain clothes.

Hart jumped up and said; 'do sit down Mr.Löeb; would you like a coffee?' Günther responded; 'I vant a solicitor to represent me in dis ridiculous charge.'

'After we have had a little chat with you sir; regarding your reason for being in the country and you giving us some satisfactory answers, we will be happy to oblige,' said Hart.

'I haf nothing to say, until I am represented;' insisted Günther.

'That's a pity;' responded Hart; 'because we are prepared to help you providing you are willing to help us with our enquiries.'

'I am here on business.' insisted Löeb.

Hart smiled sweetly; 'did your business include strangling a Mossad agent Herr Löeb?'

'I know nothing about that ridiculous accusation;' shouted Günther, 'I vant a solicitor, it iss my right.'

The other man spoke up; 'at the moment you are looking at a life sentence for killing that man; it would be wise to co-operate with us at this stage otherwise once your solicitor arrives we cannot do anything for you.'

It began to dawn on Günther that he was in an impossible position; abandoned by Von Richter; banged to rights by the British; he had little wriggle room other that to throw himself on the mercy of his interrogators.

CHAPTER TWENTY FIVE

Löeb's shoulders sagged and his head went down as the defiance went out of him. He might as well try and save his skin; it was obvious that no one else was going to.

'What are the Teutonic Warriors planning?' asked Hart.

'I vill tell you that ven I know vot help you vill gif me;' retorted Loeb.

'If you give us the information we want, that would go towards shortening your sentence; also we would change your identity and put you on a protection scheme.'

'The alternative is that you will be sentenced to life imprisonment without parole. The implications of his situation spurred him on to open up to the interrogation and within two hours the whole plot was laid bare. 'Have you got any of this Mn43 with you?' asked Hart.

'Ya, Here in in mine flight bag.' Löeb said eagerly. Hart blanched; 'you mean to say that you've been carrying the damned stuff around with you?'

'It iss only activated ven added to vater;' replied Loeb.

Hart rang for someone to retrieve the flight bag and arranged to have it sent to Portland Down for analysis. Loeb was returned to his cell to await the arrival of his brief and Cooper and Hart reviewed the situation.

'We have to get onto the UN so all countries can be warned of the danger these crazy bastards are about to unleash.'

'Once they release the stuff into the water supply people are going to die like flies.'

'Presumably there must be an antidote?' said Cooper, 'otherwise everyone including the Nazis would be infected?'

'Yes we need to get our hands on it as soon as possible;' mused Hart, that's where Mossad comes in; they have agents working on this case already in Argentina.' He got up and stretched; 'Look you had better get back to Norwich I've got a lot of phone calls to make after I've seen the Home Secretary and you have plenty to do at your end.'

CHAPTER TWENTY SIX

Foley looked up as Cooper entered the office; 'Hallo Guv; 'Paper Clips' has been looking for you.'

Cooper groaned; it looked as if he was on the carpet again; 'OK I'll go and see what I haven't done now.'

He knocked on the Inspector's door and entered; Grant was poring over a document and looked up; 'Ah there you are Cooper, you are getting extremely elusive these days'.

He motioned to a chair and Cooper sat down apprehensively awaiting whatever Grant was about to accuse him of.

Amazingly Grant seemed quite affable, even managing a rather bleak smile.'

'I have received a glowing report from Mr. Hart regarding your input to this case and a request for your co-operation as it progresses.' 'Obviously this must not interfere with the investigation of Sir James's murder; but as you say the cases are probably interlinked, so you have my blessing in the matter; well done Cooper, keep up the good work.'

Cooper came out of Grant's office in a daze; this was the first time in living memory that he had received more than a grudging comment on his successes!

He sat at his desk absently going through his in tray when he noticed a neat brown parcel with the W.D.motife on it.

Opening the accompanying letter he saw it was from the lady that had provided him with the previous information on Sir James War Record. There were two addresses of relatives of the soldiers who went into captivity with the MP during the

Desert Campaign. This was great news; at last here were two further sources of enquiry to follow up; one was an address in Kent the other was closer to home; in fact it was about two miles from Marston. Cooper whistled softly, this was indeed a turn up for the Book.

'Come on Foley, you need some fresh air, you're beginning to look decidedly peaky.'

Foley beamed; 'you mean to tell me guv that I'm going to actually be involved in real police work?'

'You bet;' grinned Cooper grabbing his raincoat; 'we're going to interview a suspect.'

They arrived outside the address which was one of a row of council houses. It looked extremely run down with an old car in the front garden and weeds proliferating all over the area.

'Wonder when they're going to make the jungle picture,' quipped Foley?'

Cooper knocked at the front door; there was the sound of slow dragging footsteps and the door was opened by a slovenly looking woman.

She peered suspiciously at Cooper and said; 'whatever it is you're selling I don't want any.'

Before she could elaborate he showed his warrant card and said: 'I'm Detective Sergeant Cooper and this is my colleague Constable Foley, may we come in?'

Muttering something unintelligible she opened the door; a miasma of body odour and cooking fat hit their nostrils as they followed her down the hall and entered what passed for a living room. The three piece suite had been covered in some sort of chintz material the pattern of which was no longer recognisable due to the accumulated dirt and grease.

On the table there was a Vodka bottle with about a third left in it and the paper on the walls was in the process of migrating to distant climes.

'Would you like a cup of tea?' the woman asked.

'Er no thanks," said Cooper hastily, "we've just had one at the station.'

Cooper noticed a faded photo on the mantelpiece of a man wearing a shirt and shorts; he picked it up and said to the woman; 'Is this husband?'

'No that was my brother Ernie; he was a Desert Rat, he died last year he never got over bein' a prisoner of War.'

CHAPTER TWENTY SEVEN

The hair on the back of Cooper's neck rose; he knew instinctively that he was close to finding the answers he was looking for.

'Have you heard of Sir James Farrington Wells?' he asked.

She looked up at him with those drink sodden eyes and said; 'course I have; he's that MP that lives in Morston.'

'Didn't you know he had been murdered?' said Cooper watching her face closely; was that a momentary glimpse of fear that came and went in her eyes? Recovering she said; 'No I don't read the papers or go out much.'

That he could believe; probably the shop and the off license were her only ports of call.

'How long have you lived here Mrs.Clarke?' he asked.

'Since that layabout husband of mine cleared off with another woman.'

At this point she reached for the bottle and poured some more vodka into her glass.

'Would you mind if we had a look round?' asked Cooper.

'Yes I bloody well would.' she said belligerently, 'what are you looking for anyway?'

Ignoring the outburst Cooper replied; 'would your brother have owned a pistol when he was in the War?'

Again that look of fear; she definitely was hiding something, he pressed her.

'Could he have left it here after he went to the Middle East?'

'You can get out of my house now;' she shouted, 'coming in here and asking questions about my poor brother, I'll make a complaint about you I will; you have no right to come in here and accuse people of having guns and things.'

This tirade went on for a while and Cooper realised that he would have to get a warrant to search the place. He made his excuses and followed Foley outside.

'Phew, she's scary Guv and no mistake; no wonder her old man did a bunk, who could blame him?'

'I don't think it was all one sided;' said Cooper, 'I can't help feeling sorry for her; the bottle is probably the only solace she could find.'

CHAPTER TWENTY EIGHT

He obtained a Search Warrant the next day and together with a Forensic Team returned to the house and began to examine every inch of it. After two hours he began to despair of finding anything incriminating; but then one of the Forensic team found a loose floorboard in the back bedroom. It was duly removed to expose a space containing an old shoe box, in which they found a Webley Service Revolver and some .38 ammunition wrapped in an oilskin cloth.

The gun had been oiled and cleaned recently and was in full working order.

On confronting Mrs.Clarke with the gun Cooper was treated to another tirade interspersed with language a Navvy would have blanched at.

He waited patiently until she ran out of steam and said quietly; 'How do you account for this gun being hidden in the house?'

"Don't know anything about the ******* thing:' she slurred her words, obviously she had started early.

'Who else lives here?' asked Cooper.

'Nobody; I'm all on my own you stupid f****** copper.'

'Well, stupid or not I'm going to arrest you on suspicion of being an accessory to murder; we'll have another chat when you are in a fit state.'

It took two burly constables to take her out of the house struggling and screaming obscenities to a waiting Police van. Nothing further came to light in the house and Cooper called off the Forensic team. Driving back to the Station Cooper remarked to Foley;

'She knows a lot more than she's telling, perhaps when she sobers up we will be able to get more information.'

'In the meantime Forensic may get some prints off the gun that will help us to establish who pulled the trigger when Sir James was killed.'

'So you don't think it could have been her?' said Foley.

'God no; she would have missed even at close range in her usual state; apart from that I doubt whether she could have walked the two miles to Marston; no there's someone else involved and that's our task, to find who she's protecting.'

CHAPTER TWENTY NINE

Kossof had been keeping Von Richter under surveillance for some days and watched as yet another Mercedes swept through the gates of the Nazi's property. Obviously there was something big happening; but what? a meeting perhaps to further their evil intentions; he had to get inside the place, but how.' There was a high wall around the building and he had glimpsed several tough looking men patrolling the grounds; some with Doberman dogs on a leash. He started the car and drove back to the office where he conferred with Wolfisch.

It was decided that a subterfuge was necessary to gain entrance to Von Richter's place. Therefore Kossov would attempt to gain entry posing as a tradesman of some sort.

He arrived at the gates later that morning posing as a plumber; complete with a small van full of tools and dressed in overalls he showed a business card to the gatekeeper.

The man examined the card carefully and looked hard at Kossov; 'I've had no instructions to let anyone in to mend a leaking faucet.' he said, 'I will ring the house.

'OK,' Kossov replied looking relaxed; but in reality his heart was racing; he watched the man as he came back from the phone; to his surprise the man said; 'I can't raise anyone at the house at the moment; I guess it will be alright, carry on to the rear of the house and call one of the staff to show you where the leak is.'

Kossof couldn't believe his luck and carried on down the long drive, rounding a bend the house came in sight; it was a large place with sash cord windows and an impressive façade. He drove around to the back and parked, taking out his bag of tools he knocked on the back door and a woman wearing an apron opened it and looked quizzically at him.

He grinned and showed her his card; she glanced at it and said, 'You'd better come in.'

As they walked down the flagstone floored hallway she asked; 'do you know where the leak is?'

'Yes, I was told it is in the upstairs bathroom' she showed him to a flight of stairs and said; 'when you get to the first floor follow the corridor till the fourth door on the left, that will be the bathroom you want.'

He thanked her and walked up the stairs; so far so good he thought. On reaching the bathroom he knocked and walked inside, it was empty.

He got out several tools and a blowlamp which he distributed around the floor, then he went to the door and looked out into the hall, it was empty so he slipped out and made his way to the other end where another flight of steps went down. He quickly descended stopping to listen; hearing the faint sound of voices coming from further down the corridor he quietly made his way towards the sound.

He arrived outside a paneled door and put his ear to it, he recognised Von Richter's voice; the man was addressing an audience.

'We are used to disappointment my friends; but this setback has been particularly damaging to the cause; Löeb has failed in the sacred mission that he was charged with and will pay the ultimate price for his incompetence.'

'However all is not lost and a new agent will be sent to Britain to complete Operation Phoenix.'

'Once the supplies of Mn43 have been distributed to our agents there the rallying cry will go out all over the world and once again the Third Reich will rise from the ashes of history to resume its rightful place as World Government.'

'Then we can build a world that the Fuhrer would have been proud of; a world populated by the Master Race.'

At this point there were roars of 'Seig Heil; Deutchland über Alles.' from the audience.

Kossov shuddered, It was the same old cry, the same mad rhetoric heard a thousand times, the same fixation that had lead to World War and millions of his race being subjected to terrible humiliation and death. These people never change, and now they were preparing to eliminate the rest of mankind on the altar of their sick ambitions. He stole away and returned to collect his tools and drove back to Buenos Aires with a heavy heart.

CHAPTER THIRTY

Cooper entered the interview room, glancing at his watch he switched on the tape recorder and sat down; looking across the table at Mrs.Clarke and her Brief he recorded the time and those present. She looked terrible; obviously the withdrawal symptoms from her habit were playing on her nerves and she constantly fiddled with her bracelet.

Cooper said kindly; 'once we've got this interview over Mrs.Clarke I will see that you get medical attention.'

'She muttered something unintelligible and continued to finger her bracelet.

Her Brief interrupted, 'It is obvious that my client is in no fit state to answer questions at this time and I demand that she be seen by a doctor.'

Cooper answered coolly; 'Mrs Clarke was seen by the Police Doctor this morning and was in his opinion fit to be interviewed Mr.Whellam.'

Turning to the unfortunate woman he smiled sweetly; 'I'm sure that you will give us all the help that you can in furthering our enquiries Mrs. Clarke.'

'As you are aware the gun found in your house is the murder weapon used to kill Sir James Farrington Wells; now I know that you did not kill him; but I also know that you know who did and for whatever reason you are shielding them.' 'In Law, this makes you an accessory before and after the fact and subject to be charged along with the murderer.'

'The only way that we can help you is if you disclose information that leads to the arrest of the guilty party or parties; do you understand?'

She looked up and then dropped her eyes and mumbled; 'No Comment.'

Cooper turned to Whellum; 'Look, for Heaven's sake can't you persuade your client that it is in her best interest to help us?' 'You can imagine what the rest of her life behind bars will do to her; she will not cope.'

'I have advised my client not to answer your questions as it may well jeopardise her case when it is brought to Court!' answered Whellum primly.

Cooper sighed: 'Look Mr. Whellum, I am sure that you think you have your client's best interests at heart; but by helping us now we can advise the Court that she has been co-operative and this will go in her favour when it comes to sentencing.'

Mrs.Clarke suddenly straightened up and gripping the edge of the table said vehemently; 'you're wasting your breath if you think I'm going to help you lot; I'm not goin to grass up my'…, here she pulled up short and lapsed into silence.

Cooper made several attempts to get her to complete what she was going to say, but she remained silent. He could see that further interrogation would be a waste of time so he terminated the session and Mrs.Clarke was returned to her cell. Cooper returned to his office mulling over what she had left unsaid, it obviously was someone close to her that she felt she had to protect; a close relative or even a friend. On the face of it both seemed unlikely; there was certainly no evidence of anyone else living at her house, and as for a man friend that seemed a remote possibility.

'Foley, I've got a job for you; get over to the Council houses where Mrs Brown lives and do a bit of sleuthing for me will you?'

'Sure Guv,' what particularly do you want me to find?'

'Whether Mrs. Brown has any next of kin would be helpful; also any close acquaintances.' replied Cooper.

'OK Guv, can I have a chitty for my expenses?'

'On your bike Foley and don't push your luck; I expect a report on my desk by this afternoon.'

Foley left the office struggling into his mackintosh and muttering darkly about 'slave drivers'.

Richter's Mercedes sped along the road to Buenas Aires at a steady 80 kilometres an hour; Kossov was finding it hard to keep up in his little van. He had been tailing Richter in the hope of discovering the source of this Mn43 stuff that had been mentioned at the meeting. It had to be manufactured at some Pharmaceutical Laboratory and he was hoping that this was Richter's destination. As they reached the outskirts of the city Richter turned off onto a dirt road lined with poplar trees and proceeded towards a large complex, raising a cloud of dust as he traveled towards it. Kossov pulled off the road into a group of trees as the Mercedes was parked outside the main building. He watched through field glasses as Richter entered the building and then looked at the legend on the sign over the entrance; 'Murkel Pharmaceuticals'. This had to be where the deadly weapon was made; he slipped out of the van and cautiously made his way towards the complex.

Richter was in conversation with Murkel; 'Have all the quotas of the virus been delivered Herr Doktor?'

Murkel was evasive; 'er, we have had some difficulties with our deliveries Excellency.'

Richter became angry; 'Dumkorf, 'your incompetence is a threat to the whole operation; timing is vital to the success of this enterprise; I will give you a week to rectify your mistake or you will be replaced.'

The Doctor cringed and began to protest his loyalty to the Cause.

Richter stared at him with contempt, 'it has always been the intellectuals who have let us down with their empty promises and impractical ideology, you will carry out my orders or it will be the worst for you.'

With that he turned on his heel and stormed out of the room, leaving Merkel ashen faced and trembling with fear.

Kossov had managed to work his way round to the back of the buildings where he found the entrance to the underground boiler and generator level, he slipped inside and went down a flight of steps into an area of lagged pipes, a huge generator and boilers. The noise was deafening and he narrowly missed bumping into a man working on some piece of machinery; fortunately the man had his back to him and he managed to get past without being spotted. At the end of the room there was a door to the stairs; he cautiously went up to the next level. A plaque on the wall announced 'To the Laboratories;' looking through the glass he perceived that the corridor was empty and he entered. He looked into the first room which was empty and slipped inside; there were some white coats and rubber boots inside a cupboard and he found a set that fitted; at least he would look the part if challenged. Armed with a clip board he sallied forth into the corridor again and began walking down checking each door as he went; he wasn't really sure what he was looking for, but he would just have to play his luck. Half way down he noticed a Fire Alarm button on the wall with a baton beside it. He picked it up and smashed the glass, pressing the button to set off the alarm.

As the alarm started ringing people began to pour out of the laboratories and make for the emergency exits. In the resulting chaos he slipped inside the nearest section and examined the work area. Each bench had an isolated glass cubicle with rubber sleeves and gloves for working remotely on whatever was inside the cubicle. There were Petrie dishes inside several containing cultures of various bacteria which presumably were being studied or developed. Quickly he moved over to the work bench and checked the various labels on the packets stacked neatly together; the label on the top one read Mn43.

CHAPTER THIRTY ONE

Foley swore softly as the rain started; he still had two miles to go before he reached the Council Houses. By the time he got there it was coming down in stair rods; he parked his bike and ran down the path of the first house and pounded on the door. It was opened by a small woman with a crab apple face and twinkling blue eyes.

'Come in young man you look as if you've fallen in the brook.' she led him in to the living room, took his wet coat and hung it near the fire.

'I know what you need; that's a nice cup of tea; I was just about to make one for myself when you knocked.'

She bustled off to the kitchen and Foley heard the reassuring sound of the kettle boiling.

She brought him a large mug of tea and said; 'get that down you and then tell me what it is you want to know.'

Foley was amazed; his jaw dropped open and when he had recovered he asked: 'how did you know I was making enquiries?'

'About Mrs.Brown;' she finished his sentence for him, 'it was easy I saw you with your boss the other day when you took her away.' Her eyes twinkled again: 'It's been quite exciting lately with all that's going on; we don't get much entertainment around here.'

He sipped his tea and then told her what he was trying to find out about Mrs. Brown's relations."

She considered for a moment and then said; 'have you traced her son?'

'We didn't know she had one.' admitted Foley, 'she's not been very co-operative.'

She laughed; 'She's a bit of a Tartar when she's had a few, particularly when it involves him.'

'Where is he living?' Foley enquired.

'I'm afraid that is a question I can't answer; she's very tight lipped at the best of times and more so about Henry.'

'He used to live with her, until he was sent to prison; that was two years ago; he did nine months for affray and when he came out he went to live somewhere near Birmingham.'

'That's about all I can tell you I'm afraid.'

Foley finished his tea and thanked her profusely for her help, his coat had dried out somewhat and donning it he went outside; the rain had stopped.

CHAPTER THIRTY TWO

Kossoff moved swiftly down the corridor towards the door to the boiler room; the way he had entered the building.

Traversing the cellar he cautiously opened the door leading to the outside and looked out. The staff from the laboratories was gathered outside the main entrance for an official communiqué; he could also hear the sirens of approaching Fire appliances. Time to go, he slipped out of the door and keeping a watchful eye on the crowd went around the building and made for the trees at the back, eventually reaching his car. He turned the opposite way to whence he had come; he didn't want to be seen by the Fire crew as they arrived. Back at Headquarters still wearing his white coat he was the butt of one or two wisecracks; ignoring the banter he went into Walfisch's office and laid the package in front of him. The man's eyes widened, incredulously he gingerly picked it up and looked at Kossoff.

'You've actually managed to get some of this stuff? How did you manage it?'

Kossoff swelled with pride; 'it wasn't easy, but I used my initiative and picked it up in one of the labs.'

He went on to tell Walfisch the whole story and the man listened intently; 'you weren't followed here Daniel?' he asked.

'No, I got away without being noticed; they were too busy dealing with the imaginary fire.'

Walfisch checked his watch; 'I must get this sample on the next flight to Tel Aviv, our scientists will want to examine it.'

'What are we going to do about the laboratories?' said Kossoff, 'something has to be done to stop them manufacturing it.'

'It was a pity that you didn't manage to set fire to it in reality;' sighed his boss.

'I could always go back there with a thermite bomb;' suggested Kossoff.

CHAPTER THIRTY THREE

Cooper looked up as a bedraggled Foley came into the office;
'Good God boy I asked you to gather some information
not attempt to swim the Channel.'
'Very droll Guv;' replied Foley, to the accompaniment of
a hearty sneeze.
'Get that wet coat off and sit near the radiator;' said
Cooper kindly.
He sent down for some hot soup from the canteen and waited
till Foley had consumed it.
Foley began to steam as he dried out; Cooper had to avert his
eyes as he began to debrief him in an effort not to crack up
with mirth. As the boy relayed his interview with
Mrs.Plunkett, Cooper realised that Foley had indeed brought
him some vital information.
'Well done lad.' exclaimed Cooper, 'I think you've put us
on to the final stage of this case.'
'We've still got to find out where the bloke lives;' said
Foley.
'No problem;' said Cooper, 'his Parole officer will have
details of his last address; come on Foley let's get off to
Birmingham.'
'What about my tea,' protested Foley?
'We'll get some sandwiches on the way;' Cooper called
out as he ran down the stairs.
The rain held off as the car tore down the A14 towards
Cambridge; Cooper hummed tunelessly as he drove; he was
elated by the thought that the end of this murder was in sight.

Foley had excelled himself this time and Cooper would make sure that 'Paper Clips' would be notified of his part in the case. They weaved through the busy traffic in the centre of Cambridge and got onto the Huntingdon Road; the rain decided to start again and the rhythmical thump, thump of the wipers moving the water off the screen became a constant companion on the journey. Cooper looked across at Foley; the lad was fast asleep; he'd had a busy day.

CHAPTER THIRTY FOUR

During the enquiry regarding the false Fire Alarm at Merkles Laboratories it was discovered that a container of Mn43 was missing. Richter was incandescent; he berated Merkle for being incompetent and demanded that there should be an internal enquiry and a review of the firm's security;

'We have reached a critical phase in the planned attack and I will brook no incompetence at any level.' Here he looked at the wilting Scientist and said with feeling; 'No one is irreplaceable Herr Doktor; please remember that as you and your staff redoubles your efforts to complete your part of the plan.'

Merkle grovelled; protesting his undying loyalty to the Cause and promising Richter that all would be well. Richter was unimpressed; he selected one of the younger Technicians to monitor Security in the labs and to report to him daily.

'There will be no more lapses in efficiency Merkle and I will hold you personally responsible.'

With that he swept out of the meeting, leaving the Director in a state of utter panic. The newly appointed Head of Security began to beef up the patrols outside the buildings, drafting in more men and dogs; also having a series of light systems covering the ground around the building to make things difficult for any would be intruder. He kept an eye on Merkle and reported his every move to Richter. Ramón Agrero was an ambitious young man and had seized this opportunity handed to him by Richter with both hands. Coming from a poor family in a run down part of Buenos Aires,his family had scrimped and saved in order to send him to school. He had worked hard and eventually won a Scholarship to University; where he gained a Degree in Science. He had managed to get a job with Merkles as a Lab Technician with little chance of promotion. Now he had power over both the Company and his boss and he was determined to make the most of it. He picked up the phone to make his daily report to Richter.

CHAPTER THIRTY FIVE

Foley awoke just as the car came into the outskirts of Birmingham; he yawned and stretched.

'Back in the land of the living?' said Cooper; he looked tired.

'Yes Guv; where are we?'

'Just coming into 'Brum', keep an eye out for a Police Station, I need to ask where the Probation Office is, said Cooper tersely.

They found the main Police Station; parked up and went in; Cooper showed his Warrant Card to the Desk Sergeant and he gave them details

'The Probation office is just off the Dartmouth Road, but I doubt you'll find anyone there now,' he said; 'I'll just give them a ring on the off chance.' they were in luck; one of the staff had been working late and agreed to see them.

Thanking the officer they hurried back to the car and made their way to the address given them. The Probation Office had an air of depression about it; the windows were dirty and the paintwork was peeling; it had certainly seen better days. However the man who greeted them belied the impression of despair; he was in his late thirties with an unruly mop of ginger hair an engaging smile and an air of optimism.'

'Hallo Detective Sergeant Cooper;" he said reaching out to shake his hand; 'and this is?' he said indicating Foley.

Cooper made the introduction and they were ushered into Tony Large's office.

'What is it I can do for you?' he asked, putting one of his crepe soled suede shoes on the desk.

Cooper explained; Large frowned and said: 'I'm afraid he's not one of my cases; it's probably one of Lennie Braithwaite's.'

'Is it possible to contact him?' asked Cooper.

Large grimaced; 'unfortunately he's on holiday in Austria till next weekend.'

Cooper's face fell, 'Ive just driven over 160 miles to get the address of this guy so I can arrest him for suspected murder; surely you could sneak a peek in his file for me?'

Large thought for a moment, then he smiled and said; 'what the hell, I might as well be hung for a sheep as a lamb.'

He jumped up and unlocked one of the steel filing cabinets and took out a brown manilla file.

He laid it on the desk and said; 'I'm just going out of the office; you won't look in the file, will you?' so saying he winked and left the room.

CHAPTER THIRTY SIX

Cooper scanned Henry Brown's file; his career of crime had commenced early in his life; starting with Borstal at the age of fourteen, he worked his way through various corrective institutions until his last stretch in Pentonville, for GBH.

He was released two months before Farrington Wells was murdered, so he could be put in the frame for that, unless he had a cast iron alibi. Cooper felt that there were sufficient grounds to arrest him and charge him with the crime.

Brown lived at an address in Smethwick; Cooper looked at his watch, it was twenty past seven.

'I think we'll find some digs for the night and call on Brown early tomorrow morning Foley.'

'Why not go now Guv; strike whilst the iron is hot?' said Foley looking puzzled.

'Because our friend is violent and as we have no back up we could lose him; he will be in bed when we call and the element of surprise should be in our favour;' answered Cooper.

They spent the night in a small Commercial Hotel nearby and Cooper arranged for a call at five the next morning.

Driving through the mean streets of Smethwick as the night gave way to dawn

Foley yawned and rubbed his eyes; 'Do you really think that Brown will come quietly Guv?'

'I haven't the faintest idea; we'll just have to play it by ear;' said Cooper squinting at the street signs as they went by them.

'Ah; here we are.' he said turning into shabby looking terraced close; 'keep your eyes open for number 23 Foley will you?'

The street light outside the house was still on as they stopped and got out of the car. It was cold and a slight mist hung over the area as they walked down an alley running between the houses. There was a wooden fence at the back of the house with a gate; Cooper tried it, it was locked.

'Looks like we'll have to climb over Foley;' Cooper grinned as he said it; he knew that Foley wasn't keen on getting his clothes dirty.

CHAPTER THIRTY SEVEN

Cooper slid the blade of his knife under the kitchen window and eased the catch open; raising the window he climbed in, followed by Foley, who inadvertently put his foot in the soap dish and skidded into the sink. There was a commotion upstairs and a large man in his underwear gripping a pair of trousers came down the stairs and made for the front door. Cooper made a grab for him and received a punch in the eye for his trouble, causing him to loose his footing as Foley fell over him.

The man ran up the street and disappeared down an alley; 'Damn and Blast it,' said Cooper nursing his eye and pushing a winded Foley off himself.

He jumped up and gave chase; but by now the man had made himself scarce, obviously the street was empty. He walked disconsolately back to the house, where the unfortunate Foley was recovering his breath.

'Are you alright Foley?' he asked.

'I will be when I get my breath back;' said the lad hoarsely; 'I'm sorry Guv, he must have heard the noise when I fell in the sink.'

Cooper gingerly felt his eye, it was swelling nicely.

'Come on Foley we had better go to the 'Nick' and report what's happened; they can get an APB going for our friend Mr. Brown, I doubt he has got very far.'

They arrived at the Station and the desk Sergeant looked at Cooper's eye;

'Forgot to duck Sarge?' he enquired.

'Spare me the funnies.' said Cooper, 'we've just been

assaulted by a murder suspect who is also on probation; he is now on the run in your Parish.'

'Will you get an APB out on a certain Henry Brown who is wanted in connection with a murder in Norfolk?'

When the necessary information had been circulated Cooper and Foley drove back to Norwich to face the music after their Keystone Cop episode in 'Brum'; Cooper could just imagine the reaction of the Uniformed Branch, they would have a field day with it.

CHAPTER THIRTY EIGHT

Simon Kossof re-read the fax from MI5 and threw it down in exasperation; who the Hell did these people think they were?

The words of the message burned themselves into his brain. 'Obtain sample of Mn43 Antidote and forward to us for analysis,Treat as most urgent.' Hadn't he already risked his life getting the virus? Now these clowns wanted him to go back into the laboratories again.

He stormed into Walfische's office seething with resentment; 'Have you seen this?' he asked.

Gabriel sighed; 'Yes Simon I have; unfortunately I have received similar instructions from Tel Aviv; the Brits have us over the proverbial barrel.' 'I cannot let you go in there on your own; I have arranged back up, there will be a team with you this time to deal with whatever the place has in the way of Security.' 'Your task is to get your hands on the Antidote and nothing else; they will ensure the mission is carried out.'

'Surely we will lose many of our Comrades in such an action; not only that, but the Argentinian Government will come down on us like a ton of bricks?'

Gideon smiled sadly; 'You may be right, but we have to try; the whole world may be depending on us for their very survival.'

'They have never been too worried about our survival in the past said Simon bitterly.

'We have our orders from Israel; that should be enough Simon;' Gideon said softly, 'the team will meet this afternoon to work out a plan and we go tomorrow night.'

With that he closed the ledger on his desk and stood up; putting on his jacket he turned to Simon; 'coming for something to eat?' he said.

CHAPTER THIRTY NINE

'Why didn't you work with Birmingham Police Force?'"said Grant looking accusingly over his half glasses; 'surely it would have been sensible to involve them in the arrest.'

Cooper looked hurt; I was following up a lead that had been given to Cadet Foley here in Norfolk sir and saw no need to involve the Local Branch there.'

'Well as things turned out you would not have lost him if you had Cooper; and another thing; putting an inexperienced trainee in such a dangerous situation was, to say the least, foolhardy.'

"Cooper looked crestfallen; 'yes sir, I have to agree; I'm afraid that my enthusiasm rather outweighed my caution, fortunately the lad wasn't hurt.'

'Let us hope that Brown is apprehended quickly; so that a veil can be drawn over the whole unfortunate episode;' said Grant briskly, 'now Cooper perhaps you will be good enough to convey my appreciation to Foley for his excellent detection skills in obtaining the information regarding this case.'

Cooper left Grant's office somewhat relieved that the 'wigging' had been relatively low key.

He told Foley about Grant's comments on his detective work and the lad glowed with pleasure.

'Perhaps I'll get more involved in real Police work now Guv; paper work is all very well, but it doesn't exactly get the blood racing.'

'I think you've had enough excitement recently Foley; apart from that how would the paper work get done?'

'We could get a Woman PC to do it.' said Foley brightly.

'That would almost certainly guarantee that no work would get done at all; you would be too busy mooning over her,' grinned Cooper momentarily forgetting his badly bruised eye; 'Ouch.' he said as his hand flew to the tender organ.

'Told you to get some steak on that eye.' said Foley, swaying expertly out of the path of a file traveling in his direction.

CHAPTER FORTY

Von Richter paced up and down the carpet in Murkel's office; things were not going well; Not only were they having difficulty persuading certain politicians to join in Operation Phoenix, but the distribution of Mn43 was falling behind schedule; despite his appointment of Ramón Agrero as Overseer of production. There were mutterings amongst the rank and file of the Teutonic Warriors about inefficiency and delay which were aimed at him; it had even been mooted by some that a Leadership Election should be held. He had to head off this mutinous faction before things got out of hand.
To this end he had decided to make an example of Murkle and take over the day to day running of the business himself.

The previous day Merkle had met with an 'accident' on his way home; a truck had come out of a side road hitting Merkle's BMW which had unfortunately collided with a large tree. Merkle had to be cut out of the vehicle, but despite treatment at the roadside he died on the way to hospital.
The truck, (which was stolen), was set on fire and the driver had disappeared before the Services arrived on the scene. Agrero came into the office and Von Richter outlined the situation; 'You will now be in charge of the production and distribution of Mn43; workers will be ordered to work longer hours in order to meet required schedules until further notice.' Ramón was unable to resist a smirk of satisfaction at his speedy promotion and thanked Von Richter profusely.

In response Von Richter said icily; 'remember that success will be suitably rewarded, but failure will incur a very different reward.'

The young man felt a cold chill run down his back at these words; perhaps this sudden promotion was not as desirable as he first thought. To add to Richter's woes he had heard nothing from his agent in London for the last few days; despite urgent messages sent. It looked as if the man had been apprehended by British Security; nothing seemed to be going right.

CHAPTER FORTY ONE

There had been a sighting of Brown at the Watford Gap Service Station; he was probably making for London where he could lose himself in the crowds. Cooper grimaced as he read the fax from Birmingham; it would be like looking for a needle in a haystack if the man succeeded. This case had proved to be so frustrating, particularly as although they knew who had killed Farrington Wells, he had slipped through their fingers due to Cooper's over confidence. Now he would have to rely on the good offices of the Met' in apprehending the felon for him. He decided to ring Tony Large at the Probation Office in Brum' to see if Brown had any contacts in London. It was a long shot, but worth a try; otherwise it could take forever for the Met to get round to looking for him.

The familiar outgoing voice of Tony answered; 'Hello Detective Sergeant Cooper, good to hear from you again, how can I help?'

Cooper explained and asked if there was anything in Brown's file regarding contacts.

'I'd better put you over to Lennie, as it's his case;' Tony said, 'just a moment while I put you through.'

A moment later a voice with a thick Birmingham accent answered; 'Hullo; how can I help you like?'

Cooper went through his request again, there was the sound of papers being shuffled and then Lennie said; 'apparently he served time with a character called Reg Varney here in Brum, he was referred to the Probation office in Stepney after getting out.'

'Do you have their number?' asked Cooper.

'Just a mo'I'll look it up for you,' answered Lennie; there was the sound of papers rustling and some muttering then he returned to the phone and gave Cooper the number.

Thanking him Cooper rang off feeling that he was getting somewhere at last,.he picked up the phone and began to dial the number Lennie had given him.

CHAPTER FORTY TWO

Kossof switched off the engine of the Mini Bus and picked up the night binoculars. Sweeping across the forecourt of Merkel Laboratories he made out two guards with dogs patrolling the area.

He turned to the Back up Group Leader and informed him; 'it will be difficult to approach whilst the dogs are at the front of the building, we must wait till they are taken round to the back.'

The leader grunted in agreement; 'I don't fancy being torn to pieces by a couple of German Shepherds Simon.'

The bus was parked in the trees that fronted the building hidden from sight, but they had to somehow reach the building without being seen, otherwise a fire fight could ensue; attracting attention from the authorities. It seemed an age before the patrol moved away from the front of the building and Simon and his men emerged from the bus and cautiously made their way towards the building. Leading them to the door of the Generator and Boiler installation he tried the door; it was unlocked. As they slipped silently inside they were aware that the lighting was on; Simon raised his hand to stop the group's progress.

'There is a man tending the boilers somewhere about;' he whispered, 'he will have to be dealt with.'

They fanned out in search of the man; but were unable to locate him; then one of the men found him fast asleep behind the warm boiler. Simon heaved a sigh of relief and beckoned the men to follow him to the staircase accessing the Laboratories. Peering through the glass in the door to the hallway he was alarmed to see a white coated man coming out of one of the units; obviously the staff was working overtime; this really had put the cat amongst the pigeons.

CHAPTER FORTY THREE

Cooper sat in the Police van as it sped towards Brown's current address in Stepney. There were half a dozen burly Coppers supplied by the Met to ensure that the man didn't escape again. He had his Superintendent to thank for organising this co-operation from the Flying Squad, apparently he and the Commander went way back. The van pulled into a quiet cul-de-sac and the driver turned and said;
'There's a passage through to the street we want, taking in the back ways to the properties, where half of you can gain access to the garden.' He went on; 'The rest of you can deploy at the front of the place ready to go in when the door comes down; Good Luck and watch out for weapons.'
The team climbed out of the van and made for to the passageway.
When everyone was in position two large officers with sledgehammers broke down the door and the team poured into the house yelling, 'Police stay where you are.'
As they rushed up the stairs there was the sound of breaking glass; they entered a bedroom to find a weedy looking individual cowering in bed and a large jagged hole in the window. Looking down into the back garden Cooper perceived Brown bleeding profusely being handcuffed, he was stark naked.

CHAPTER FORTY FOUR

The arrests having been made and clothes found, the pair were arraigned and charged at Bow Street. Brown was charged on counts of assaulting an officer in the course of his duty and breaking his bail conditions and Varney for harboring an absconder. Cooper was given an interview room and Brown arrived still handcuffed between two officers. He began the interrogation regarding the murder of Farrington Wells after cautioning Brown. At first the man refused to co-operate, but Cooper persisted and eventually he began to respond. He admitted shooting the MP and Cooper asked him what his motive was.

Brown became animated; 'cos he was a murdering bastard, that's why.'

'Can you be more specific?' said Cooper.

'A mate of my uncle told me all about Sir bloody Farrington Wells, he was with him during the war and they were both captured and put in a German prisoner of war camp in the desert,' replied Brown.'

'What happened then?' prompted Cooper.

The man continued; 'apparently there were several plans to escape, but the Germans always knew in advance and were ready and waiting to shoot the soldiers.' 'My uncle told him he reckoned that Farrington Wells was giving the Germans all the details.'

'How could he possibly know that?' interjected Cooper.

'Cos Farrington Wells was given special privileges and was always on good terms with the Germans.'

'Hmn, that's hardly proof that he was a traitor,' said Cooper, 'was there anything else that aroused your uncle's suspicions?'

'Yes, Uncle Ernie reckoned that his escape was a put up job, his mate told me that the lorry that took the waste away was always searched at the gate before it was allowed out of the camp, but the time he went out there was no inspection!'

Knowing the facts he had already gleaned about Farrington Wells Cooper could see that Brown's uncle's observation was sound. He switched the interview to the details of the murder.

'Can you fill me in with the details of what happened on the night that you confronted and killed him?'

'Yeah; I'd gone to my uncle's funeral the previous week and was feeling pretty mad about the fact that Farrington Wells was still alive; so I asked mother where his gun was, saying that he had promised it to me.' 'She handed it over and I checked it out to see if it was in working order, which it was.' 'There were half a dozen rounds of ammunition so I took it with me and walked to Morston.'

He stopped; 'Look all this talking is making me throat dry; could I have a cup of tea?'

Cooper turned to one of the constables; 'would you mind getting Mr.Brown a drink?'

The man duly went off and returned with a mug of tea.

Brown had a swig and resumed his confession; 'I walked down the path and knocked on the front door, cocking the pistol and putting it behind my back.'

'Farrington Wells came to the door and when he saw me he told me to clear off, saying that he wouldn't tolerate visits from scum like me.'

'I can still see the look on his face when I put the gun in his face and pulled the trigger.'

'The gun made a hell of a noise and I ran off after I'd put a white feather in his hand, quick as I could before any of the neighbours could come out and spot me.' 'A week later I was banged up for another job and spent the next eighteen months in Birmingham 'Nick.'

Cooper heaved a sigh of relief; the man had been honest about the case and saved a lot of time.

He said quietly; 'you realise that you will be charged with murder Mr.Brown?'

'I know;' he said, 'but if I had to do it again I would; that man was responsible for the deaths of his own men, he was a traitor and deserved what he got; I got rid of a bad man Mr. Cooper.'

'I'm afraid that I can't go along with you;' said Cooper quietly, 'as an upholder of the Law it is my duty to charge you, whatever I may think of your motives; thank you for being honest with me, these officers will look after you now.'

CHAPTER FORTY FIVE

Kossof realised he had to amend the plan of attack now they had to deal with workers being in the laboratories. The risk of casualties had greatly increased due to this unforeseen factor Fortunately they were equipped with CS grenades which would temporarily disable anyone who confronted them, but it would make searching for the antidote for the virus more difficult. He ordered the team to don their gas masks and check their weaponry. Looking out at the corridor all seemed quiet; he opened the door and the team fanned out to cover him as with two combatants he opened the door to the first laboratory and looked in. So far so good, it was empty; quickly he examined everything on the tables; there was no sign of an antidote. He turned to the store cupboards and rifled through them, again without success. He jerked his thumb towards the door and they went on to the next Lab.

Again he drew a blank; there was no sign of what he was searching for. Just then he heard a commotion outside in the corridor; as he came out of the door he saw a person in a white coat struggling with two of the team who were attempting to overpower him. Without further ado he ran across and hit the guy on the temple with the butt of his pistol.

> The man fell to the floor out like a light; Kossof examined him; 'he's only stunned, he said, tie him up and put him in the empty Lab.'

Having disposed of this threat without seemingly having aroused any further diversions they pressed on down the corridor. At the next door Kossof put his ear to the door; there were the sounds of conversation and movement. He signaled to the team to have their CS gas canisters at the ready, threw the door open and they stormed in to the room. The Lab technicians froze into an unlikely tableau; except for one young man who reached across the bench towards a button.

Kossof raised his pistol and said; 'pressing that button will be your last act; do not try it or I will shoot.'
Ramón Agrero stepped back from the bench; he was a brave young man, but he was not a fool, this man obviously meant what he said and Ramón had no inclination to become a martyr. Kossof searched the room again without success; turning to Ramón he said;
'We are here for the antidote to Mn 43 and will not leave without it, you can save yourself and your colleagues by telling me where it is.' Ramón glanced at a large safe right at the far end of the laboratory; 'Good;' said Kossof; 'who knows how to open it?'

CHAPTER FORTY SIX

When Cooper arrived back at Bethel Street Brown's arrest had already broken and he had to fight his way through the throng of Newsmen and Photographers. When challenged to give details he shouted over the hubbub; 'there will be a Press Call as soon as it can be arranged.'

On arriving at his office the phone was already ringing, picking up he recognised the voice of Tony Hart;

'Hello Dan, congratulations old boy meticulous police methods do work after all.'

'Seriously though many congratulations, I should think you're pretty chipper about it?'

Cooper chuckled, 'well put it this way Tony at least it's got a certain person off my back.' 'Changing the subject somewhat; how is the Teutonic Warriors situation going?'

Tony grunted; 'we are awaiting news from Argentina, Mossad are supposed to be sending a sample of the antidote.'

'I suppose that now I've got my man you won't need me Tony?' said Cooper rather wistfully.

'Don't worry Dan, I'll keep you updated as things progress; there may be ways you can still help,' said Tony mysteriously; 'got to go now old boy, talk to you later.' with that he rang off.

Grant sent for him half an hour later for a debrief;

'Well done Cooper; your perseverance has paid off at last.'

Cooper didn't appreciate the last few words of that sentence.

'It was a difficult case Sir, requiring patience and a little luck.'

'Well surely Cooper you don't rely on luck to solve a case?' said Grant with raised eyebrows; he continued, 'anyway a Press Call has been arranged for this afternoon at two thirty; I suggest you don't mention luck to the Press, they would have a field day with that.'

CHAPTER FORTY SEVEN

Kossof stood over the elderly Lab Technician whilst he laboriously fed in the numbers of the combination of the safe. As the door was opened Kossof pushed the man aside and knelt down to examine the contents. There were several stacks of plastic containers inside the safe, but the only clue as to their contents was encoded on the packages.

He turned to the man and said; 'which are the ones containing the antidote?'

The man shuffled uncomfortably and mumbled; 'I am not sure Señor as I only move what is given to me.'

Kossof's eyes narrowed: 'do you take me for a fool; why would you be given the combination to the safe if you were only an underling?'

'I am telling the truth Señor, I have the combination as I am directed to fetch whatever is required in the main laboratory or the Warehouse.' replied the man.

Kossof turned to the other prisoners: 'do any of you know which of these the Antidote is?' 'I want an answer now or there will be consequences.'

No one replied and he realised that time was not on his side; he had to make a decision.

'Take the lot out of the safe; we will have to move them all.'

The packages were stuffed into the knapsacks that his men were wearing and after cutting the telephone cables in the laboratory they locked the staff inside and made their way back to the boiler house.

CHAPTER FORTY EIGHT

The Press Call was packed; not only with the locals, but also with hacks from the Tabloids and some Freelance journalists all clamouring for information. What with that and the continual popping of flash photography it was bedlam until Inspector Grant raised his voice above the hubbub.

'Gentlemen, if you wish to hear the information that we have for you, I insist that you be patient and give Detective Sergeant Cooper a chance to speak.'

Immediately questions were being fired from all directions.

Grant raised his arms and waited till the noise subsided sufficiently for him to respond.

'There will be a chance to ask questions after the details have been presented; now I will hand over to Sergeant Cooper.'

Cooper went through the facts of the investigation and the salient points that had led to the arrest of Brown for the murder. He omitted to make any mention of the MI5 investigation into Farrington Wells connection with the Nazis; it was up to the Security Services to deal with that 'Hot Potato.' The question session began with fairly routine subjects regarding the MP's background and War Record; then a large man with a choleric complexion shouted from the back of the room.

'What about his alleged association with the Germans during the War?'

There was a sudden hush and everyone turned to look at the accuser. He sat back with his arms folded and an air of triumph at having delivered this bombshell.

Cooper recognised him at once; it was Mick Malony a renegade freelance renowned for digging up the dirt wherever he could find it. Where had he got his information; had someone at MI5 leaked it? There was obviously a source, either there or in the Force.

Grant stood up; 'May I ask where you obtained this allegation?'

The man smiled smugly and said; 'I refuse to reveal my sources, as you well know Inspector.'

'You may well be proceeded against if it turns out to be untrue.' said Grant.

'Well I'm prepared to risk that Inspector as I got it from a most reliable source; anyway the freedom of the Press must be respected mustn't it?'

CHAPTER FORTY NINE

After the Press Call was over Inspector Grant discussed Malony's 'Bombshell'.

'Where has this man got his information?' asked Grant; 'it seems there has been a leak, either in the Force or perhaps the Security people.' 'I don't think so Sir;' responded Cooper, 'more likely it had something to do with the break in at Farrington Wells's house.'

'Do you think that Brown carried out the break in?' said Grant.

'No, he didn't have time;; when the shot occurred he said that he left the scene in a hurry; I think that it was someone who had something to hide, possibly connected to the Nazi plot who saw their opportunity to remove any incriminating material.'

'Yes, but who?' exclaimed Grant.

'That's the million dollar question Sir: alternatively it could have been taken for gain; for instance if someone was hired to search the house for incriminating material which would show the deceased in a bad light.'

'You mean for political ends Cooper?' exclaimed Grant.

'Maybe, or more likely for gain; I think I will have to question Malony in more detail regarding his sources.'

Grant looked unconvinced; 'I don't think you will get anywhere with him Cooper; he has always stuck to his guns before when interviewed.'

Cooper grinned; 'never say die Sir, I have my ways, especially with characters like Maloney.' said Cooper, 'the fact that Malony got hold of it suggests that it was stolen for gain rather than to cover someone's tracks.'

CHAPTER FIFTY

The Firefight started as soon as the Mossad party emerged from the boiler room. Two of them were hit immediately and had to be carried as they scattered for cover, but it seemed they were surrounded.

'Make for the bus!' shouted Kossov. as he sprayed the area with his Ouzi automatic, suddenly feeling a stabbing pain in his leg he fell to the ground still firing.

A flare lit up the surrounding space and a voice from a loud hailer addressed them.

'You are surrounded and outnumbered, throw down your weapons and stand still or you will be shot.'

Ignoring the warning two of the Mossad party began running and were immediately brought down in a hail of bullets.

'Resistance is useless; put up your hands and stand still!' the voice continued; 'We will come and collect your weapons and take you into custody.'

A tall distinguished looking man stepped into the light and Kossov recognised Von Richter; he was holding the Hailer in one hand and a sub machine gun in the other.

'We have been waiting for this futile visit for some time and you have played into our hands; did it not occur to you how easily you obtained the antidote?'

'My workers played their parts very well and now we have you in our grasp.'

He turned and barked out orders in Spanish and men came forward and handcuffed the hapless Jewish fighters.

They were marched back into the building which was now ablaze with light; Kossov had to be supported by two of his captors and he could only wonder what Fate would befall him and his band at the hands of this fanatical Nazi.

CHAPTER FIFTY TWO

Superintendent Trafford gazed at the ceiling and putting his hands together he looked over them at Cooper. 'Are you sure you want to do this Cooper?' He said.

'Absolutely sir,' replied Cooper leaning forward in his chair, 'the man obtained his information from someone who is involved in this case, of that I'm sure.'

'Have you contacted MI5 about this?" asked Trafford.

"Yes, I've discussed it with Agent Hart and he's of the same opinion as me, in fact they are putting agents on surveillance of the guy as we speak.'

'So why should we commit more men if they are already dealing with it?'

'Because in the event of the leak coming from here sir, I want to be able to follow it through.' responded Cooper.

'Yes I see your point Cooper;' said Trafford thoughtfully; 'we don't want to end up with egg on our faces, the Press would have a field day with that.'

'Alright go ahead and keep me informed; pick whoever you need within reason, but remember we haven't got unlimited man power.'

Cooper was glad he had gone straight to the 'Super,' rather than Grant, he could just imagine the reaction and he certainly would have had difficulty getting the men he wanted.

Next morning he held a briefing for the surveillance of Maloney.

'What you are going to hear must not go outside this room,' warned Cooper, 'you will be working with agents from MI5 and in order to succeed complete security must be maintained at all times.'

'You will report to me each day to be given your brief and to inform me of anything you have found during your investigation.'

One of the men put up his hand; 'what are we looking for "Guv?'

'A complete report on Maloney's movements and details of his contacts,' replied Cooper. 'Also I am advising you not to discuss this case with anyone outside the squad however trustworthy you may consider them to be.'

'This case is of great National importance, anyone found divulging anything about it will be disciplined and kicked out of the Force immediately.'

As the officers were filing out Cooper called over three of them; 'I want you guys to monitor all outgoing calls from the 'Nick.'

They looked shocked; 'you mean you want us to spy on our colleagues?' said Detective Allan Groves incredulously.

'Cooper looked him in the eye and said; 'It's necessary Allan, because we don't know where this guy is getting his info and I want to make sure it's not coming from here.'

CHAPTER FIFTY THREE

The captured members of Mossad were herded into a large windowless room inside the Laboratory complex and their handcuffs were removed Von Richter stood in the doorway as the guards filtered out still covering the prisoners with their weapons.

'You will be quite comfortable in here while we decide what to do with you; but don't build up your hopes; there is no chance of you escaping; should you try to make a break for it you will be shot.'

'So farewell for the moment Gentlemen, we will be back soon to take care of you.'

He said the word gentlemen with a sneering emphasis, turned on his heel and left. The metal lined door was shut and the sounds of several locks being activated were clearly heard.

Kossov painfully straightened up, his leg was throbbing, he had lost a considerable amount of blood; he looked round at his remaining group.

'Any bright ideas about getting out of here?' he enquired.

'With no windows and a steel lined door there doesn't seem much point;' said one of the group; 'anyhow by the time we've tried they will be back to do whatever they have decided to do with us.' 'Then we had better get a move on,' said Kossov with a smile; 'there is one thing that our Teutonic friends have over looked.'

He pointed to a wire mesh grill half way up the wall; 'the air conditioning ducts.'

'It should be possible to remove the grill and crawl through the ducting to somewhere else, preferable an outside wall.'

'Give Isaac a bunk up so he can see if it will come off.'

The men gladly complied and soon removed the metal grill, exposing the dark mouth of the shaft. Forming a human wall the men entered the shaft one by one, passing Kossov up before the last man was pulled up and the grill was replaced.

In an untidy line they shuffled forward on all fours along the duct encountering blasts of warm air coming from in front of them. Coming to a bend in the tunnel they turned the corner and were confronted by a shaft going downwards.

'What shall we do Simon?' asked the front man.

'Can you see anything at the bottom Isaac?' queried Kossov.

'No but I can hear what sounds like machinery working down there;' the man replied.

'Good;' exclaimed Kossov, 'it must be the generators in the basement.' 'What sort of depth is it Isaac, can you see?'

'About ten feet to the bottom I think!' said the man.

'Right; can each of you remove your belts and fix them together, so we can pull Isaac up if necessary,' called Kossov, down you go Isaac and have a look round.'

The man lowered himself over the edge and let go; they heard him thud on the floor below.

He was gone a few moments and returned with the news that it was indeed the basement.'

'Good, down you go men and let's get out of this accursed place.' They went down the shaft one by one.

CHAPTER FIFTY FOUR

So far the surveillance of Maloney had produced little of any worth; it was almost as if the man knew he was being watched.

'It seems as if he has a contact who's feeding him information from an official source.' said Cooper.

'I don't mind admitting that I have a gut feeling that it could be from here.'

'Could be from anywhere old boy,' said Hart laconically; 'we are having an internal investigation as we speak.'

Cooper was amazed at how lightly Hart seemed to be taking a possible serious breach of security, but then he always displayed an unflappable manner, so perhaps it went with the territory? He concluded the conversation with;

'Anyhow, the sooner we find whoever the 'Mole' is, the sooner we will be able to track down Maloney's source.'

He rang off and headed for Grant's office; he knocked and went in.

A look of annoyance flitted across Grant's face as he looked up; 'I wish you would ring first Cooper.'

Cooper observed a large graph spread out on Grant's desk with multi coloured lines interweaving across it.

'I am just finishing a flow chart of duty rosters for the forthcoming year Cooper, essential to the smooth running of the department, so everyone will know exactly what is expected of them.' 'No haphazard, impetuous hunches, but clinically meticulous information.'

Cooper leaned over the chart and said innocently, 'aren't there thirty days in November sir?'

Grant went a delicate shade of puce; grabbing the chart he crumpled it up and threw it on top of the filing cabinet.

'What was it you wanted to see me about Cooper?' Grant spat out the words as if they were vitriol.

'About the internal Security check that the Superintendent requested sir' responded Cooper without the vestige of a smile.

With a great effort Grant gained some self control; 'Er yes Cooper, I was going to contact you about that; what progress have you made?'

'None sir; I came to request your permission to proceed with it forthwith; I certainly wouldn't presume to act without your authority.'

'It wouldn't be the first time if you did Cooper;' retorted Grant.

Having been somewhat mollified at having scoring this reposte Grant waved a dismissive hand and said; 'carry on Cooper, try not to disrupt the routine of the station.'

As Cooper left he looked back in time to see Grant spreading his chart out again and reaching for the Tipex.

CHAPTER FIFTY FIVE

Gabriel Walfisch wearily packed his belongings into a carpet bag; he had been replaced by Simon Kossov, but he was not bitter. Tel Aviv had blamed him for the failed raid on the laboratory and he had to admit they were right.

'I'm getting too old for the cloak and dagger business;' he murmured aloud.

'It was not your fault Gabriel,' said Kossov who was standing behind him, 'no one could have foreseen the ambush; they were waiting for us when we arrived.'

'I was in charge and have to accept the responsibility;' remarked Wlfisch sadly; 'including the death of our three comrades; it is only right that I should go.'

'The work needs a younger man, someone with an agile brain and the courage to act; in fact they have made the right choice as far as I am concerned Simon.'

He turned around and held out his hand; Simon grasped it and embraced the old man.

'I shall miss your wise counseling Gabriel,' he said; 'what will you do now?'

'Retire to a kibbutz and grow melons most probably,' said the old man with a wry smile.

'Surely you will do more than that?' asked Simon; 'what about your music, of course you will continue to play?'

Walfisch shrugged; 'my fingers are getting stiff and my violin is not friendly with me now.'

He straightened up and smiled; 'my good friend I shall miss you and life is not going to be the same; but rest

assured I shall often be thinking of you and the good
work we have done together.'
He turned away quickly so the tears would not show, picked
up his carpet bag and made for the door, leaving Kossov
feeling that the void in his heart would take an age to fill.

CHAPTER FIFTY SIX

Hart phoned early that morning with news of the arrest of Malony's source, which turned out to be an old lag by the name of 'Fingers' Marcovitch; so called because of two missing fingers on his left hand which he had lost due to being over generous with some nitro whilst trying to crack a safe. He had been arrested by Essex police whilst trying to rob a stately home where he had been disturbed by the incumbent millionaire who held him at gun point till the police arrived. Whilst being charged he asked to have a second offence taken into consideration, namely the Farrington Wells break in.

Cooper was ecstatic; 'I knew it had to be a professional job Tony; what's going to happen to Malony?'

'He will be charged with aiding and abetting a felon and withholding evidence of a crime, his goose is well and truly cooked.'

Cooper rang off feeling cock a hoop; 'will you get me the desk at Chelmsford Nick Foley if you please.' He spoke to the desk Sergeant and asked for the detective in charge of the arrest of Marcovitch.

'Hallo; D.S. Martin speaking;' the voice was rasping with a distinct local accent,'Can I help you?'

'You most certainly can;' replied Cooper happily; he then went on to explain his involvement in the case and asked if he could go over to interview Marcovitch.

Martin was reluctant at first until Cooper offered to share information connected to the contents of the safe; he then became keen to co-operate and an appointment for a meeting was arranged. Cooper strode around the office humming to himself, much to Foley,s annoyance.

'What have I done to deserve this discordant outburst Guv?'

Cooper stopped humming and smiled radiantly; 'I am humming Foley because I am happy; surely you can appreciate that?'

'It's not the happiness Guv, but the noise it creates that I object to.' retorted Foley.

CHAPTER FIFTY SEVEN

Boris Markovitch was an interesting character; born of Russian émigrés he was a small dapper man. Originally he had worked for a famous safe manufacturer in the City. However he developed a weakness for gambling and got caught up with the criminal fraternity who exploited his expertise to their advantage. When Cooper interviewed him he was slumped in a chair looking decidedly sorry for himself.

Before turning on the tape recorder Cooper introduced himself and had a chat with him; 'Can I get you anything Mr.Markovitch, a coffee perhaps or cigarettes?'

'It is thoughtful of you Mr.Cooper, but I am afraid that as this is my third offence, things will go badly for me and I will receive a long sentence.'

'That depends on what you tell me;' replied Cooper; 'you may be aware that I have been involved in the investigation of the murder of Sir Farrington Wellswhose house you burgled?' 'If you can tell me what was in the documents that you took from his study you will not only be helping me, but also providing information which will help to prevent an international conspiracy.' 'The judge may take a more lenient view of your crime and possibly shorten your sentence if I inform the court of your co-operation.'

Markovitch looked down at the floor and remained silent for a few minutes.

Looking up he said; 'your offer is very tempting Mr. Cooper; but what guarantee can you give me regarding protection?' 'Mr.Maloney warned me that if I grassed he had very powerful friends who would not hesitate to have me killed in the event of my talking to the police.'

'We would of course put you on our relocation programme,' countered Cooper. 'You and your family would be given new identities and relocated where you would not be known.'

'Alas I have no family and I have always lived in London,' replied Markovitch sadly; 'I'm afraid that I am a creature of habit Mr. Cooper and would find it very difficult to adjust to a new way of life.' 'In any case I am afraid that I did not read the contents of the documents I took, but just handed them over to Mr.Maloney as he requested.'

Cooper's heart sank; he had no reason to doubt the sincerity of what the man was saying; he certainly had nothing to gain by lying.

He thanked Markovitch for his candid response and rang the bell for the escorting officers to return him to his cell.

He would have to wring the information out of Maloney; knowing the man he knew he had a hard task ahead of him.

CHAPTER FIFTY EIGHT

Simon Kossov looked around the room at the anxious faces of his fellow agents. This was his first briefing since Gabriel had relinquished his leadership of the Argentinian branch of Mossad. He wished that Walfisch was still here, the man always seemed to impart a reassurance that David did not posses at the moment. Taking a deep breath he launched into his address;

'I don't need to tell you that our last operation ended in failure and the loss of three friends that we all miss.'
'There must be no repeat of this, the next operation must be meticulously planned and executed down to the last detail.' 'Time is not on our side as the Teutonic Warriors are well advanced in their proposed attack on the rest of the world.' 'Therefore we have to hit them fast and completely destroy the laboratories and what they contain,' 'It is certain that supplies of the virus are already being distributed and individual countries will have to deal with this themselves.' 'However it is only fitting that ours is the main task to eliminate this nest of vipers once and for all to avenge our people who were eliminated in the "Final Solution.' 'The plan is being finalised and should be ready tomorrow morning; in the mean time check your weapons and stand by for further orders; Thank You.'

He lit up a cigarette and found that his hand was shaking; it had been an ordeal, but he had come through. Several of the men shook his hand as they left and others nodded and smiled; seemingly his address had achieved the desired effect.

CHAPTER SIXTY NINE

It seemed to Cooper as he drove to interview Maloney that there was more to the break in than met the eye. How did Maloney know there were incriminating documents in the house? Was he informed by someone beforehand who had a vested interest in making them public and if so, why?

Arriving outside the grim exterior of Parkhurst he parked up and walked to the main entrance. After showing his ID he was taken through a series of doors to level two where the prison officer showed him into an interview room and left to fetch Maloney. When he arrived dressed in prison garb Cooper noticed a certain diminished attitude in Maloney's normally truculent manner. He was obviously finding the regime hard to deal with Cooper bade him to sit down and passed over a pack of cigarettes which the man grabbed gratefully and lit one up.

'To what do I owe the honour of this visitation?' said Maloney blowing a cloud of smoke across the table and smiling wanly; but Cooper noticed the man's eyes were wary.

'We're still trying to get to the bottom of this break in, said Cooper, and I was hoping for some co-operation from you.'

'What's in it for me?' said Maloney.

'I can't make any promises, but your co-operation should have some bearing on the length of your sentence.' said Cooper.

Maloney considered for a few moments then said; 'Alright, since I seem to be left in the lurch I'll talk.'

He went on to describe how he had been approached by a man called Wellander with a proposition to expose Sir Farrington Wells. The man gave him details of where to look for incriminating documents proving that the man had been a Nazi agent since the war as well as during it. He got the impression that the man was using an assumed name, as he seemed more British than Scandinavian. Maloney arranged for Markovitch to do the break in, but he was disturbed by a police patrol and did not have time to open the safe.

However what Markovitch managed to find was damming enough for Maloney to write the story and get it published.

He received a handsome check from Wellander and that was the last contact he had with the man.

Maloney leaned back in his chair, looked Cooper in the eye saying, 'and that's about it Mr.Cooper, that's all I know.'

Cooper switched off the recording machine and turning back to Maloney said' 'Thanks for your help, I'll send a copy of my report to your brief, it should help with your case. He paused; 'I don't suppose you have a phone number or postal address for this Wellander guy?'

Maloney shook his head; 'no, but I did record the meeting with him, I usually do that with contacts in case of repercussions.'

'Will you let me have it?' Cooper said eagerly.

'Sure,' said Maloney, 'it's with my belongings at reception.'

Cooper's spirits rose appreciatively as he left the interview room and made his way down to reception.

He presented the chit that he had got Maloney to sign authorising him to collect the tape and hurried back to Bethel Street to play it.

As the conversation progressed he began to realise that Wellander's voice sounded familiar under the guttural accent;

where had he heard it before?

CHAPTER SEVENTY

The truck backed slowly into the warehouse, as soon as it stopped Kossov and two other men came forward and opened the rear doors. Inside was a long wooden box bearing a stencilled message, 'Tractor Parts.' The driver helped them to lift the box out and they carefully placed it on the floor.
Kossov inserted a jemmy under the lid and prized it open.
The interior of the box was packed with straw, which he removed revealing a torpedo shaped object painted in a drab green colour.
'What the devil is that Simon?' asked one of the men.
'It is the means of removing the threat of the doomsday weapon.' he said solemnly. He went on to explain the function of the weapon. 'It is a wire guided missile developed by the Russians and supplied to the Egyptian Army.' 'However we have had it modified by filling the warhead with Thermite, so in effect it is an incendiary device.' 'So hopefully if it does its job it will be difficult for the Argentinian Government to pin the blame on us.'
'When are we going to use it Simon?'asked the other Mossad operative.
'In three days time there will be a new moon and conditions should be ideal to launch it;' responded Kossov, 'now let us get this thing secured and ready ourselves for our 'Final Solution.'

CHAPTER SEVENTY ONE

The night was overcast, favouring Mossad's proposed attack on the late Merkle's Laboratories. From the safety of the tree line facing the buildings Kossov went over the launch procedure of the wire guided missile once more. It was vital that he got it right for there wouldn't be another chance to destroy the place if he got it wrong. The missile was launched from the shoulder, requiring another person to support the weapon during firing; once on it's way it could be controlled with radio signals from a small transmitter.

'Are you ready?' he murmured to his colleague; his finger began to tighten on the trigger, when someone came out of the front door of the building and walked briskly to a car parked nearby and got in.

It was Von Richter.

Damn! Simon felt a wave of anger well up inside as the Mercedes flashed up the road with its headlights blazing.

The one person that he really wanted to destroy had escaped retribution, for now at any rate. Pulling himself together he concentrated again on firing the missile.

CHAPTER SEVENTY TWO

The rest of that day Cooper kept running the tape over and over, becoming evermore sure that the voice of Wellander, despite the guttural accent, was familiar.

When he arrived home Sheila noticed he was preoccupied as his responses to her conversation were minimal and vague

She sat down in front of him and looked into his eyes; 'Where are you at the moment Dan?' she said, 'it's a sure bet you aren't here.' 'She looked up at him and said; 'I seem to recall that we agreed that you would leave your problems at the office.'

'Sorry love, I've got a nagging problem with a case at the Station; but you're quite right, he said with a grin.' 'Let's change the subject,' what's for dinner?'

Sheila playfully aimed a blow at him which he caught; 'isn't that typical of a man; always thinking of his stomach; if you must know its chicken casserole.'

'I thought I could smell something burning.' he quipped, ducking as she took another swing at him. He jumped up and headed up the stairs to have a look at his son and heir, blotting out any further thoughts about familiar voices.

CHAPTER SEVENTY THREE

Simon Kossov pulled the butt of the rocket launcher hard into his shoulder and squeezed the trigger, there was a slight delay and then a roar as the missile sped towards the laboratory complex. His colleague guided it from the remote box he held in his hand and it went straight through a window on the ground floor. There was a brilliant flash of light as the thermite exploded and the building became a raging inferno. Momentarily he felt a qualm of conscience for the people inside, but when he thought of the consequences of the Nazi plan to flood the world with Mn43 he was reassured that he was doing the right thing. Quickly disassembling the launcher they made their way back to the van and drove off, leaving a scene behind them that Danté would not have recognised in his wildest dreams. By the time the local Fire Brigade arrived the place was a smouldering ruin and they could do little except damp down what was left of the buildings. Back at Mossad headquarters the group had a de-briefing from Kossov whilst outside the sound of wailing sirens as the Argentinian authorities indicated the panic that their action had caused. The remaining parts relating to the missile had been buried in woodland on the way back from the fire, so hopefully there would be nothing remaining that could connect the group with the outrage. Simon knew that they would be the first suspects, there would be a visitation by the Argentine Security Police.

CHAPTER SEVENTY FOUR

Cooper was still no further forward in tracing the owner of the voice on the recording he had taken from Maloney! All he knew at the moment was that he had heard the voice before; it had the same timbre and pitch of someone he had conversed with during this investigation. Grant had already chided him at the lack of progress in closing the case and at the moment Cooper had no idea where to go from here; he had to solve the mystery of the identity of whoever it was on the tape before he could move on.

Foley looked up from the files he was studying and looked over at him; 'What's up Guv? You seem a bit preoccupied at the moment.'

'I certainly am Foley,' responded Cooper, he went on to explain the problem, finishing with; 'so you see until I can figure out who this guy is I'm stymied.'

Foley thought for a while and then said; 'what about voice recognition?'

Cooper frowned; 'what on earth are you talking about lad?'

'Well apparently the recording studios evaluate music by running the sound waves on a screen, so the engineers can make adjustments to a tape.'

'You never cease to amaze me Foley, where did you get this information from?' said Cooper.

'A friend of mine works at a Studio in Norwich Guv;' the young man replied.

'Do you think he would run this tape through their system?' said Cooper eagerly.

'Don't see why not Guv; would you like me to give him a ring?'

'Yes I would and thank you for the info; this could be a break through in the case.'

'A thought just struck me;' said Foley, 'it's all very well getting the tape analyzed, but you need to find a match to confirm who it is.'

'Damn,' said Cooper, his hopes being instantly dashed.

'It will need tapes of people that have been interviewed during the investigation Guv in order to eliminate them.'

Cooper groaned; 'that's going to take an age Foley.'

'Not if you recall suspects to interview about a new development and record the conversations; which you would do anyway.'

Cooper thought for a while and then brightened up: 'you're right Foley, let's get the ball rolling, we can use the tapes we already have, which will eliminate some interviews being necessary, in the meantime ring your friend and see if he's prepared to get involved.'

CHAPTER SEVENTY FIVE

Kossov stood amidst the wreckage of his office; the Security Police had been thorough in destroying every piece of useful equipment they could lay their hands on. They obviously knew Mossad had been responsible for destroying the Murkel Laboratories, but without proof they had resorted to vandalising their premises. His assistant Ben Silverman came in and surveyed the wreckage;

'Mice?' he queried sardonically.

Kossov allowed himself a wry smile; 'yes mice with large boots Ben, at least they have not arrested us yet; but I don't doubt they will be back.' He moved over to the window and looked down into the busy street bustling with life; 'I must admit that I have had pangs of conscious regarding what we have done; but if we had not then most of mankind would have been eliminated by these Nazi maniacs.' 'They have to be stopped from carrying out their diabolical plans and it is up to us to do what we can to finish it.' Ben looked up from his attempt to clear up; seeing the strain on his leaders face he said;

'You had no other choice Simon, instead of condemning yourself you should instead rejoice for all the lives that you have saved by your action.'

'You are a good friend Ben,' said Kossov: 'what you say will help me to see things in a different light in time I guess, but why it that in this life we are constantly battling evil?'

'That is a question I have no answer for.' responded Ben.

CHAPTER SEVENTY SIX

Cooper gazed about him in awe as he surveyed the array of sound technology surrounding him. He and Foley had brought the recording to the studio so that the Sound Engineer could compare it to the voices of the people interviewed in the Farrington Wells case. The man sat in front of a large sound desk with a big screen over it, which had weird patterns traveling across it. As each voice was played it produced a series of waves on the screen which the technician overlaid on the tape provided by Maloney. It took the afternoon to assess all the interviews and Cooper began to lose heart as to whether this futuristic machine would be able to come up with the goods. However on the very last interview he saw that the waves matched exactly those of the suspect tape.

He leapt up and shook Foley's hand excitedly; 'you've done it lad; you've cracked it.'

Foley positively glowed with pride at the praise being showered on him by his boss, but tried not to seem too affected by it.

'Well it's all a matter of keeping up with modern technology,' he said; adopting a nonchalant pose.

'Aren't you going to see who it is Guv?' he remarked carelessly.

Cooper came down to earth and checked his list with the order of the interviews and to his amazement saw who it was that had ordered Maloney to obtain the documents.

CHAPTER SEVENTY SEVEN

Von Richter put down the phone and poured himself a stiff tot of whisky; he had just finished organising the retaliation for the Mossad attack on the laboratories. It was obvious that this was their work; the very audacity of it bore the hallmark of a Jewish venture. They had certainly severely wrecked the main part of Operation Phoenix; but fortunately a substantial amount of Mn43 had been stored at his house, as he had decided to dispatch it himself due to the slow progress of Murkel. The Jews were not going to get away with their attack; he would see to that; they would be eliminated by his operatives, several of whom had been in the Waffen SS. He had been able to recruit many willing employees from the south of the country as there were over 3000,000 Germans living in Argentina, plenty of whom were sympathetic to the cause. He drained his glass and glanced at the portrait of his beloved Fuhrer hanging over the large brick fireplace; he clicked his heels and bowed then turned to a bell pull on the wall beside the fireplace and rang for his manservant, who entered silently and awaited his masters instructions.
'Pack my things Willie; I am going on a journey shortly to England.'
'Yawol, mein Herr,' responded the retainer expressionlessly and melted away to carry out his instructions. Von Richter sat down in a high backed chair in front of the log fire and poured himself another whisky; He had decided that as the English had co-operated with their Jewish friends they should be singled out for his special attention, he would carry out the attack personally.

CHAPTER SEVENTY EIGHT

The arrest of Sir Richard Coombes took place at his flat in Mayfair at six o clock the next morning. Two squad cars pulled into the Mews and the police began to bang on his door. Sir Richard answered it wearing a dressing gown and looking somewhat disheveled; 'In God's name what do you want at this time of the morning he demanded.

The Inspector in charge of the raid read him his rights on the doorstep and he was bundled into one of the cars;

The party drove off, watched by several nosey neighbours looking from their bedroom windows. He was arraigned at Bow street and formally charged under the Defence Regulation 18B (only the second MP to be charged under this order), which covers Treasonable Acts against the State. He tried to claim immunity from arrest of a Member of the House, but the Act overrides this; however he continued to protest his innocence whilst demanding legal representation. By this time the Press had got wind of it and there were photographers and reporters thronging outside the building hoping for a scoop. Tony Hart had to fight his way through the crowd, being bombarded with questions from reporters who recognised him.

> The Inspector who had made the arrest met him in the foyer and said; 'morning Tony, we've put him in an interview room for you, but he's hopping mad and calling for his brief, I doubt you'll get much out of him at present..'
> 'I shall have to see; it's surprising what a little TLC will do!' said Hart with a grin.

As he walked into the interview room Sir Richard caught sight of him and shouted, 'I might have known you bastards were behind this farrago; I refuse to be questioned until my solicitor arrives.'

'Quite right and proper Sir Richard, it's one of the privileges of a free country you know;' said Hart ironically. 'Not that it would have been free if your lot had had their way.'   '

I have no idea what you're babbling about.' retorted Coombes.

'Don't worry Sir Richard all will be made clear to you in due course.' said Hart soothingly.

CHAPTER SEVENTY NINE

Simon Kossov glanced at the wall clock, it was a quarter to ten; he had a bad feeling, Ben should have been in the office around nine. Ben was a stickler for punctuality and normally rang in if he was going to be delayed. Simon picked up the phone and rang his number; it just kept ringing. Now feeling alarmed he put on his jacket and made for the door.

He went down in the lift to the underground car park and walked across to his car. Out of the corner of his eye he saw a movement behind one of the adjacent cars. Throwing himself down he looked under the car. He observed a pair of legs moving behind the vehicle where he had seen the movement. Slipping his automatic from its shoulder holster he aimed and fired; there was a cry of pain, then the sound of someone making their way for the lift. He stood up and was just in time to see the lift doors closing; damn. He replaced his gun in the soft leather holster under his armpit, it was still warm. Getting into his car he drove out onto the street and made for Ben Silverman's apartment with a deep sense of foreboding.

Ben lived on the other side of the city near the Football Stadium as he was a keen Soccer fan. Parking up, Kossov got out of the car and ran across the leafy street into the entrance to the apartment block. Climbing the stairs he reached the door of Ben's apartment; it was ajar. He gently pushed the door open and silently entered the hallway, stopping he drew his gun and listened; the place was silent as the grave.

Fortunately he had been many times to the place so he knew the layout and headed for the bedroom. The door was wide open and Ben was hanging off the bed, he had been shot several times in the chest. Simon was devastated; he and his friend had been through so much together for the Cause and it had all ended in this assassination. It was not difficult to guess who was behind it, after all they had destroyed the Nazi's Chemical Weapon laboratories and this was obviously a vendetta to eliminate Mossad's operatives in Buenos Aires. He phoned Samuel, their secretary, and told him to warn the rest of the team what had happened and to disperse until further notice. Replacing the phone he carefully wiped his finger prints off it; he had no desire to be interrogated by the police, they had a reputation of gross brutality, especially with political prisoners.

CHAPTER EIGHTY

Cooper was in conversation with Tony Hart regarding the arrest and interrogation of Sir Richard Coombes.

'We've thoroughly searched his house and turned up a file containing correspondence from a certain Von Richter in Argentina.' Apparently Coombes has been a 'Sleeper' since before the War and now has been activated.'

'We have uncovered evidence that he was also influenced by Mosely and visited Germany several times on international friendship visits before hostilities started.'

'If you hadn't had the idea of checking his voice, we probably would never have found him.'

'Hang on Tony,' protested Cooper, 'it was my assistant Foley who had the idea; I just followed it through.'

'Well he is to be congratulated,' said Tony, 'you have a bright lad there it seems.' 'One more thing, the last letter from Von Richter indicated that he was coming over to England to see Coombes at his home.' added Tony.

'Did it mention the reason for the visit?' asked Cooper eagerly.

'Unfortunately not;' replied Hart, 'but I'm sure it doesn't bode well for us.'

'Finally I come to the main reason that I rang you; I've got a confession to make Dan, I had a word with your Chief asking if you could be seconded to our surveillance team, the reason being that your help in this case has been exceptional and I would like you to be in at the kill.

'What did he say?' asked Cooper anxiously.

Tony laughed; 'I'll let him tell you all about it, I have no desire to steal his thunder, but I think you'll be pleased.'
'That's all for now, give my regards to your lovely wife and that boy of yours; see you soon, cheerio.
'Cooper slowly put the phone down with all sorts of thoughts running through his mind; what would Sheila say about him gallivanting off for who knows how long? Also it would further aggravate his relationship with Grant, which was already at very low ebb.
'To Hell with it.' he said out loud.
Foley looked up from his desk; 'with what Guv?'
Ignoring the question Cooper smiled and said; 'Tony Hart was very complimentary about your idea to use the sound equipment to identify Sir Richard Coombes's voice.'
Foley visibly swelled with pride; 'did he really say that Guv?'
'Foley, I am not given to making false statements, at least not in front of Authority.' grinned Cooper,' of course he did and I thoroughly agree with him; now nip down to the canteen and see what culinary delights you can summon up.'

CHAPTER EIGHTY ONE

Von Richter settled back in his seat in the Business Class cabin as the mighty 747 climbed into the evening sky. The sun was setting behind the pink cumulus clouds as 120,000 pounds of thrust pushed the mighty plane up in to the stratosphere. No doubt, he thought, a lot of the technology for this leviathan of the sky came from the research on aerodynamics done by America's German Technicians captured after the War. He smiled wryly; proving once again we are the Master Race, he thought. He had changed planes at Frankfurt and was now winging his way towards England.

He opened Der Speigel and scanned through the headlines; it was the usual thing; the Russians were making things difficult again. They had started to build a wall between the already divided Germanys; fools, did they really think that would stop Germany from re-uniting? Things would have been very different if they had not been beaten by the Russian winter and that fat fool Goering failing to get supplies through to Stalingrad. He had personally seen his storm troopers still clad in summer uniforms freezing to death for the want of warm clothing and food. How did Päulus expect the German Army to fight in those conditions? Von Richter had seen defeat coming and he had broken through the 'Ring of Steel' surrounding the city together with a small band of his men by crossing the frozen lake at night. As they walked through the Russian waste lands during the terrible winter weather, one by one the men succumbed to the conditions and by the time they reached the Polish border Günter was the only one of his team left. Now here he was again conducting a one man offensive against the old enemy; he would settle the score between them once and for all by removing their Nation from the equation. He was looking forward to meeting Sir Richard once more; they had first met when a Trade Commission from Britain visited Argentina. They discovered that they had a great deal in common, both politically and ideologically. Coombes was not happy with the way that Britain was being treated by the United States as a 'dogsbody' and exploited by American business; he felt Britain's Role in the war had been played down by them in order to diminish Britain's position in the world order. He had seen Sir Stafford Cripps humiliated by having to beg for aid as Britain had been bankrupted by the war. Von Richter had found much fertile ground to persuade Sir Richard that he had been fighting on the wrong side and there was a way to right many of these wrongs by throwing in his lot with the Teutonic Knights. He also put him in touch with Farrington Wells as his mentor and informant. Now that all the other operatives had either been eliminated or failed, Coombes was Von Richter's last hope in helping to carry out operation Phoenix. He looked out of the window and glimpsed the white cliffs of Dover as the giant bird banked and changed course for Heathrow.

CHAPTER EIGHTY TWO

Superintendent Trafford waved Cooper into a chair and said affably: 'I expect you know what this is about Cooper?'

'Yes Sir I have a pretty good idea,' Cooper replied. 'Hart has explicitly asked for your co-operation in this matter as you have been involved throughout and I agreed to release you under his direction until the case is brought to a conclusion.' 'I have cleared it with Inspector Grant, despite his concerns about shortages of manpower.' here he allowed himself a deprecating smile. He continued; 'apparently MI5 are awaiting a certain person arriving in this country in order to contact Sir Richard Coombes.' 'They have his home under surveillance and want you to be available for further developments.' 'As Sir Richard's Property is located in Northumbria I am seconding you temporarily to the Newcastle Constabulary.' 'Superintendent Anderson is a contemporary of mine; we were at Hendon together.' 'He is a stickler for discipline, but you'll find his bark is worse than his bite, now you'd better go and pack; there's a travel warrant for you at the desk, so good luck Cooper and keep me informed won't you?'

They shook hands and Cooper ran down the stairs to collect his warrant, went out to his car and set off for home with his heart singing with excitement

Sheila was baking and looked up as he came through the door, pushing a stray lock of her hair away from her face she left a streak of flour across her forehead.;

'You're home early Dan;' she said, more as a statement than a question.

Couldn't stay away my love; he murmured nuzzling her ear; especially as I see you're hair is turning white through neglect.'

'What?' she said disengaging herself and rushing to the mirror; seeing the flour streak she turned and shook her small fist at him; 'I might have known it was a figment of your warped imagination.'   "

'Anyhow what brings you back home in the afternoon; it can't be uncontrollable passion?'

He drew her to him and kissed her tenderly; 'I have to go to Newcastle for a while love.'

'Is it to do with this murder case you're covering?' she said.

'Indirectly;' he replied, 'I'm working with Tony.'

'Is it dangerous?' she said looking up at him with those beautiful brown eyes.

'No more so than usual,'" he said, 'just a routine surveillance.'

'That's what you said when you went to Turkey and look what happened!'(See Final Score).

He smiled broadly and said; 'come on upstairs and help me pack.'

CHAPTER EIGHTY THREE

Von Richter's flight touched down at Heathrow just after midnight and half an hour later he cleared Passport Control and collected his overnight case from the Carousel. He had arrived under a false name, assumed when he fled to Argentina, he was now Senór Cardosa . As he walked through the Reception Hall towards the Exit he saw a man standing at the barrier carrying a placard with his name on.

He made contact and gave the man his case to carry and they went out into the rain to a Jaguar parked at the entrance.

'Did you have a good trip sir?' the man said respectfully.

'Yes thank you;' replied Von Richter brusquely, 'is there a drinks cabinet in this car?'

The driver opened the rear door and pointed to the cabinet built into the back of the front seat; ' sir you'll find a good range in there.'

He poured himself a stiff whisky and settled back into the capacious rear bench seat as the car pulled out into the exit lane and headed north. Reaching the A1 the driver picked up speed and they were soon cruising effortlessly at seventy miles an hour towards his destination, he was looking forward to meeting Sir Richard once again, he would be very useful in advising him about reservoirs in the area where he could place the Mn43 capsules. Soon the constant hum of the engine lulled him into a doze; the composure of his face gave the impression of someone without a care in the world.

CHAPTER EIGHTY FOUR

Cooper caught the afternoon train for Ely and changed again at Birmingham Central for Newcastle. By the time his train steamed into Newcastle Main it was dark and raining. He caught a taxi at the rank outside and gave the name of a Motel near the Main Police Station where he would spend the night. Once he had settled in he rang Sheila;

'How's the son and heir?' he enquired.

'I've just got him off to sleep!' she said wearily, 'he's been playing up ever since you left, wanting to know where Daddy's gone.' 'I hope he's not going to keep that up till you come back; otherwise I shall be a nervous wreck.'

'Don't worry love; this shouldn't take too long; we are waiting for this guy to arrive and as far as we know he has no idea we've arrested his accomplice.'

He was to regret this statement later due to unforeseen circumstances.

Next morning he walked to the Police Station and introduced himself to the desk sergeant.

The man seemed unfriendly and looked him up and down before saying; 'Ah canny see what you've been sent here for Detective Sergeant, we've got plenty of detectives of our own like.' Cooper looked up and smiled sweetly; 'I'm only obeying orders Sergeant, since you feel so strongly about it perhaps you would like to take it up with my Superintendent, I have his number here;

otherwise I suggest you do what I'm doing and that is mind your own business.'

'Now where is your Super's office please?'

He took the lift up to the third floor and knocked on the door marked Superintendent Anderson.

An authoritarian Scottish voice called out 'Come in;' it was more of an order than a request. The man seated behind a large desk was reading a file; he looked up briefly and said; 'I'll be with you in a minute, take a seat.' While he continued to read Cooper studied the man; He was large, but muscular; he had obviously come up the ladder the hard way; he had the nose of a hard drinker and close set eyes, his hair was crinkly and parted in the middle of his head, he had a close set mouth and a jutting jaw; not a man to cross by the look of him.

'So you're the darling of MI5 are ye?' the man said thrusting out his jaw belligerently.

'I told your Superintendent we didnay need ony help frea other Forces, but he played the Security Department card so I had nay choice in the matter.' 'This has no gone down well wi ma officers; they feel insulted that they are to be led by someone frea the South.'

Cooper was silent for a moment and then said quietly; 'with all due respect sir, I didn't come here to take over the investigation, but my orders are to liase with your squad as I have personal knowledge of the case, which actually started in Norfolk and may be able to help your men to apprehend the suspect.' 'I have no doubt that he will be interrogated by MI5 in any case as this is not only a threat to the public in this country, but also involves espionage by a foreign organisation.'

'You see sir this is a matter of life and death for every man, woman and child in the country; this man has to be caught before he can launch a deadly attack; it transcends personal feelings and boundaries, we are all involved.'

Anderson's face was a study; he was not used to be spoken to in this fashion, especially by this Sassenach interloper. Cooper could see the wheels going round in Andersons head as how to react to this information. After a pause to gather himself he put his hand up to his chin and in a more conciliatory tone said; 'Well, obviously this puts a different slant on things; we were only informed to stake out the house and apprehend this man; if what you say is true, and I'm sure it is,' he added hastily, 'you have my word that we will give you all the co-operation you need.'

Cooper smiled; 'Thank you sir; much appreciated,' he stood up; 'would it be possible for me to meet your team and discuss the way forward?'

Anderson managed what for him passed as a smile as he picked up the phone; 'Is Alec there? Will you send him up?'

A few moments later a lanky Detective Inspector named Wearmouth arrived and Anderson introduced him to Cooper.

'I want you to work with Detective Sergeant Cooper and give him your full assistance; he has a great deal of information and he is already working on the case Alec.'

The man looked quizzically at Anderson who gave him a meaningful stare.

'Now off you go and keep me informed,' said Anderson, extending a large hand to Cooper; 'Good luck to ye Cooper, I'll be following this case wi' great interest.'

CHAPTER EIGHTY FIVE

Von Richter was awakened by the driver; 'we're approaching Sir Richard's house sir, it's just over the hill.' As the car started down the steep decline the driver turned and said;
'There seems to be a police car parked outside.'
'Drive on,' commanded Von Richter, he crouched down.
As the car passed the house then looked out of the rear window; there were two policemen getting out of the car and they walked towards the gate where they were met by several other officers.
What had happened to Sir Richard; had he been arrested and the house was now being watched? 'Take me to a hotel at once and report to me tomorrow morning, there has been a change of plan.'
The driver nodded and headed further into the countryside, eventually turning into a tree lined driveway drawing up outside a large country house; the board outside proclaiming 'The Firs.' He got out and opened the door for Von Richter and followed him into reception carrying his luggage.
Booking in under the name of Cardosa which was on his Argentinean passport, he dismissed his driver and was shown to his room by the porter. He rang room service and they sent up an omelet, the restaurant being closed and the chef had already gone home. When he had finished he got undressed and climbed gratefully into bed; it had been an eventful day.

CHAPTER EIGHTY SIX

Cooper and Wearmouth drove over to Coombs's house early the next morning, where forensic were going over the place with a fine toothcomb searching for any incriminating material. If indeed there was any Coomb had hidden it well. Wearmouth introduced Cooper to his surveillance team and asked the sergeant in charge whether there had been any developments during the night;

'Quiet as the grave sir;' replied the sergeant.

'Any cars coming through here last night sergeant?' asked Cooper.

'Aye, there were one or two; it's not a particularly busy road at night.' the sergeant said.

One of the constables piped up; 'there was that black Jaguar went through when we were changing shifts, ah had'ne seen it before, it certainly wasn't local.'

'Did you see the number?' asked Cooper.

'No; it was dark and the number plate was covered in dirt; I reckon it had come a long way like and it had been raining most of the day.'

Cooper thanked the man and said to Inspector Wearmouth; 'perhaps it will be spotted in the area, there aren't too many cars of that description about.'

'I'll notify Traffic to keep a lookout;' said the Inspector, looking annoyed;

Cooper thought that the constable was going to regret not telling his Inspector first.

CHAPTER EIGHTY SEVEN

Von Richter awoke with a start, momentarily disorientated; then he remembered where he was and why. He showered and dressed, then rang down for breakfast to be sent up to his room. Finishing he got up and went to the window and looked out onto a nine hole golf course where a couple were already chasing small white balls about. The English and their silly games; he thought, they rarely took anything seriously and yet always seemed to come up smelling of roses. He turned away from the window and picked up his overnight bag, carefully removing the contents onto the bed he reached inside; moving a section of the flooring he removed a plastic container, which he slipped into his pocket. Going downstairs to reception he asked the receptionist if his car had arrived.

'Yes sir about two minutes ago, she replied, 'the driver is waiting in the foyer.' He thanked her and went out to meet him; 'have you managed to find out what has happened to Sir Richard?' he asked;

The man looked worried; 'yes sir; the story is all over the county, he was arrested by Special Branch yesterday, but no one knows what he's been charged with.'

'I can make and educated guess;' replied Von Richter grimly; 'I think in the circumstances the first thing to do is to dump this vehicle; it is too conspicuous.' 'Get something ordinary looking and come back for me.'

CHAPTER EIGHTY EIGHT

The driver returned in a grey coloured Riley; much more appropriate mused Von Richter, the last thing they needed was to be spotted by the local Police; who no doubt would already be on the lookout for a black Jaguar. He climbed into the back seat and the man handed him an Ordinance Survey map of the area. Opening it up, he began looking for large lakes or reservoirs in the area as the car drove sedately down the drive. There were two sites within a ten mile radius, namely Rothly Lakes and Fontburn Reservoir which looked likely targets. He also noticed a large wooded area close by called Harwood Forest; that would be a good place to keep the two sites under observation before proceeding with his plan. He gave the driver the co-ordinates and road details to the forest and they made their way towards it. He found a logging road which took them to the edge of the wood overlooking the reservoir and commenced his surveillance of the area with a pair of powerful binoculars he had saved from the war, to his dismay the Reservoir was swarming with people and there were sail boats on it. What was worse, there were policemen patrolling the fringes of the reservoir, obviously looking out for any attempt to contaminate the water. Just then a jeep roared up the logging road and a thick set man jumped out and advanced towards them.

'What are ye doin here?' he asked, 'dinna ye know this is Government land and ye need a permit to come on it.'
Von Richter lowered his binoculars and smiled sweetly; "I am sorry mister?..

.'Mac.Sween, and I'm the Forestry Officer,' responded the man; 'what's your reason for being here anyway?'

'Why I am an avid amateur Ornithologist Mr. Mac Sween and my colleague here kindly brought me to observe the Green Woodpeckers which I understand are abundant in this wood.'

The man looked unconvinced; 'Ye look well dressed for a bird watcher, I'm afraid that I will have to report you for trespass, there is a watch in the area for saboteurs as it is.'

He reached in his tweed jacket and took out a small notepad; unfortunately for him this was his last act on earth as Von Richter shot him where he stood.

The driver turned pale; 'what have you done sir; there was no need for that'   '

There was every need dumkorf.' retorted Von Richter, 'he would have reported us and the registration number of the car and the police would have been on our trail.'

'Commen Sie; help me to bury him and hide his car and let us get away from this place, it is not suitable for my purpose anyway, too many people, I require a more quiet site.'

CHAPTER EIGHTY NINE

Hart rang next morning with the news that after a National search the black Jaguar had been booked in the name of Cardosa from a Hire Car service in Knightsbridge. However the man who picked it up was English with a North Country accent.'

Cooper said; 'we already have people out looking for it Tony, I'll let you know when we find it.' Wearmouth came in and slumped into a chair; he looked all in. 'What's the matter Richard?' asked Cooper.'

'I'm fair wore oot man.' this wild goose chase is takin' every moment o me time like, every other aspect o crime is bein' neglected because all of our manpower has been diverted onto this one case.'

Cooper could empathize with his colleague; he had been in similar situations himself, 'I know how you feel; but the trouble is if we don't stop him a lot of people are going to die and as guardians of the peace we are the only protection they've got.'

Wearmouth nodded wearily, 'Ay I know what you say is right, but we're only human and my squad are getting' weary wi' lack of sleep.'

'I'll have a word with the Super and see if we can't get some help from the military, I believe there is a large Army camp near here?' mused Cooper.

'Why Aye.' said Wearmouth brightening, that ud be fine, why didna I think o that.'

Just then the desk sergeant came in with a message from the Forestry Commission reporting that one of their Officers

called Mac Sween had gone missing. Apparently his jeep
had been found on a logging road near Fontbourn Reservoir.
   'Come on Richard, this sounds like the break we've been
   waiting for.' said Cooper excitedly.

CHAPTER EIGHTY NINE

On arrival at the place where Mac Sween's jeep had been discovered Cooper noticed that the Reservoir was fairly close to the fringe of the forest. It was pretty obvious what had happened to the Forestry Officer. Turning to Wearmouth he said;

'I think we are going to need that extra help from the military and several dogs if we are to find this man, I think he confronted our suspect and was killed.'

He walked back down the logging road examining the tracks; fortunately it had rained recently so it was possible to see the tyre patterns. Apart from the timber Lorries there were only two other track marks and on examining the jeeps tyres. he narrowed it down to one set; these were of an unusual pattern and he retraced them down the road to the end where they had turned around. He requested photographs to be taken and copies to be issued to each constable to make inquiries about cars hired in the area.

'It's obvious that our suspect has changed cars;' said Cooper; and with any luck we should be able to track it down through the tyres.'

He asked the Superintendent to contact the local Barracks and persuade the Commanding Officer to release a couple of dozen 'Squaddies' to help with the search. Fortunately the Commander was delighted to help and four army lorries trundled into the courtyard of the Police station that afternoon containing forty 'volunteers.'Inspector Wearmouth was over the moon at this gesture of co-operation and turning to Cooper said grudgingly;

'Thanks, Detective Sergeant, I wouldn't have got them if I'd applied, you seem to be able to get whatever you want.'

'It's all about working together sir, it's surprising what can be achieved by co-operation,' grinned Cooper.

'Point taken Cooper,' said Wearmouth with a wry smile. The troops noisily disembarked from the trucks and were brought to order by a sergeant, he lined them up and and marched across to where Cooper and Wearmouth were standing, coming smartly to attention and he saluted.

Search Party present and correct sir; where would you like them deployed?'

Wermouth looked quizzically at Cooper and Cooper smiled; he turned to the sergeant and said,

'This is Inspector Wearmouth sergeant he will instruct you where he needs your men.'

'Perhaps you will excuse me gentlemen as I haven't had my dinner yet.' with that he went off to find the canteen.

CHAPTER NINETY

After several sorties Von Richter began to realise that his chances of planting the Mn43 into the local reservoirs were slim. The local Police had combined with army personnel in patrolling the area and he had decided it was time to move on to a less well guarded area. He therefore decided to try his luck over the border in Scotland, There were plenty of large stretches of water there and the population was spread more thinly in the country areas; so he reasoned that there would be less risk of being apprehended.

He packed his things and the Riley arrived at the hotel to pick him up.

The receptionist smiled as she processed his bill; 'I hope you have enjoyed your stay Señor Cardosa, perhaps we will see you again sometime.'

'It is hardly likely;' he said with some feeling, 'I shall be returning to South America very soon.'

He paid his bill and turned on his heel to walk out of Reception angry with himself for letting slip that last remark. The driver loaded Von Richter's luggage into the boot and they were off up the drive; as they neared the entrance a police car came in and headed towards the hotel

Von Richter's blood ran cold; was this just a routine check or had the police got some sort of information about him?

He turned to the driver; 'Drive like hell for the Scottish Border, we will have to change cars again once we get there, the police may have this registration.'

The driver did as he was bid and the Riley was soon speeding up the A1.towards Berwick.

CHAPTER NINETY ONE

The Newcastle police found the abandoned Jaguar in a lock up in Shield Field; the owner seemed to know nothing about it when questioned, but he was already known to the police so he was brought in for questioning. Cooper found that the old lag had plenty of experience of being questioned and after a fruitless hour and a half had to let him go, as there was nothing they could charge him with that a good solicitor couldn't override.

However good fortune came to the rescue in the shape of two Traffic Cops who had been searching the local hotels; They reported that as they turned into the driveway of the Firs hotel a grey Riley saloon was coming out; they stopped and the second cop took a note of the Registration. When they questioned the receptionist she provided them with Von Richter's details including a description, mentioning that he came from South America. Cooper and Wearmouth exchanged significant glances; this was obviously the man they were looking for. An urgent request was sent out to all Police Forces in the North of England and Scotland to apprehend the occupants of the Riley with caution as they were carrying a dangerous substance. Within two hours a report came in from the Lothian Police that the car had been seen in the centre of Berwick upon Tweed, but that by the time a police car had been summoned the car had gone. Cooper's heart sank; why hadn't the Scottish copper delayed them, till the police car had arrived to give him back up?

'I think I will have to follow his trail Alec; this case has become personal for me; this maniac has got to be stopped before he can wreak his revenge on the whole country.'

Wearmouth held out his hand; 'It's been a privilege workin' wi ye Dan; Good Luck and Good Huntin' and keep safe.'

Cooper said his farewells to the Super and the rest of the staff then went back to his digs and packed his bags. Soon he was on the next train to Edinburgh wondering where this case was going to take him.

CHAPTER NINETY TWO

Von Richter had decided to lose himself in Edinburgh, being a large city there were plenty of places in and around where he could hole up to plan his next move. The Riley came into the outskirts of 'Auld Reekie' and made it's way through the bustling traffic towards Princes Street. As usual it was full of shoppers and tourists rubbernecking at the gardens and the castle above sitting on its rocky mound. The driver turned off for the Forth Bridge and Queensferr Here Von Richter found a little guest house by the river that seemed to suite his needs and after paying the elderly landlady a month's rent in advance, he dismissed his driver, who frankly was glad to be rid of his charge. Mrs.Makenzie was somewhat puzzled why this foreign gentleman should wish to stay in a wee bothie like her's instead of one of the grand hotels in Edinburgh; he was obviously not short of a bawbee or two, judging by his insistence on paying in advance.

She called up the stairs; 'what would ye be wantin' for your dinner sir?' ah have a nice piece o salmon the noo, fresh caught this mornin'.

'That will be satisfactory;' responded Von Richter, 'I am going out for a walk and will be back in an hour.'

Von Richter's driver ran out of luck on the way back to Yorkshire. He was stopped at a police road block just North of Blaydon. He cursed under his breath as the police waved him into a lay bye; why hadn't he got rid of the Riley before coming back from Scotland as Von Richter had suggested. He was formally charged and taken back to the Station, where he was interrogated by Alec Wearmouth. Despite admitting that he had driven Von Richter to Edinburgh, he claimed that he had dropped him off in Princes Street before returning. The detective didn't believe him, but despite a long session of questioning the man refused to change his story. Wearmouth rang Edinburgh and left a message for Cooper regarding the man's apprehension;

Dan rang back two hours later; 'Great news Alec,' he said, 'has he 'coughed?'

'I'm afraid not,' said Wearmouth, 'he obviously knows more about where his boss is, but isn't sayin.'

'Von Richter's description has been circulated to every Scottish Force, so someone is going to recognise him.' said Cooper, 'but in the meantime, perhaps when the driver realises what he's involved in he'll maybe become more interested in saving his own skin.'

He rang off and requested an interview with Inspector Murray who was in charge of the search in the Edinburgh region.

CHAPTER NINETY THREE

Von Richter walked into the local newsagents and bought a map of the local area which he took back to his digs.

After Mrs.Mackenzie had served him with a generous helping of salmon with salad, he withdrew to his room and studied the local water features. There were very few lakes South of Edinburgh, but his eyes were drawn to Loch Leven on the other side of the Firth near Kinross.

'Just what I have been looking for,' he mused: it was large and probably supplied the local area with water.

He walked through to where Mrs Mackenzie was clearing the table; 'could you recommend a local garage where I could hire a car?'

She turned and said; 'Why yes sir, Dougie can fix ye up, ye'll find his place yonder doon the hill; ye canny miss it.'

After booking the car for the morning he went up to his room where he carefully slipped the vials of Mn43 inside his jacket, humming tunelessly he took off the garment and hung it in the wardrobe.

He was really looking foreword to tomorrow and the beginning of Operation Phoenix in Britain. He undressed and climbed into bed, after setting the alarm for six o clock and was soon sleeping the sleep of the just.

CHAPTER NINETY FOUR

Life for members of the Mossad team had suddenly become precarious; most of them had dropped out of sight to await things quietening down since the murder of Ben Silverman. Simon Kossov had closed the office and was working from his house up in the hills outside Buenos Aires.

He had a good view of the road winding up to the development where he lived and could check traffic coming from the city. He was in communication with Tel Aviv on his scrambler when he noticed two cars coming up the road together, they were certainly not local.

'I'll have to ring back, Shalom;' he put down the phone and took an Ouzi machine gun from the cupboard under his desk.

Quickly he moved to the back of the house and slipped out of the kitchen door; making for the trees lining the back of the estate. Due to the steep incline he could see the two cars stop just down the road from his house. Five men got out; two went to the front of the house whilst the other three hurried round to the back. Kossov smiled grimly, his Guardian Angel was working today it seemed. Ten minutes later he saw the men getting back into their cars and driving off. Carefully he returned to the house; as he opened the kitchen door there was an explosion which blew him off his feet into the garden where he lay face down motionless.

CHAPTER NINETY FIVE

Hart contacted Cooper at Edinburgh with news of a breakthrough relating to Mn42.'
They've broken down the formula of the virus and are now developing an antidote at Portland Down,' he said; 'good news eh?'
Cooper was more downbeat; 'it takes time to produce and vaccinate everyone and time is running out; we have to find this guy before he has time to activate the damn stuff.' 'What we desperately need is a lead in finding him Tony; at the moment we haven't a clue as to his whereabouts.'
'What about this driver of his,' asked Tony?
'He certainly knows more than he is prepared to divulge;' responded Cooper, 'as a matter of fact I'm going down to Newcastle to see if I can open him up.'
'Good idea old man,' replied Tony; 'talk to you later.'
Two hours later Cooper was interviewing the man Cooper switched on the recorder and sat looking at the man for several seconds before speaking.
'Look,' he said earnestly, 'I can understand your reluctance to betray your employer; but I don't think you are aware of his real reason for being in this country.'
'He was visiting an old friend;' the man began.
Cooper cut across him; 'what he didn't want you to know is that he is carrying a deadly virus with which he intends to poison the water supply in order to kill the entire population of Britain and presumably that will include

you.' The man blanched; but stubbornly stuck to his story.

Cooper sighed; 'why do you think he went on the run when Coombes was arrested?'

'If he were merely visiting a friend as you put it, what reason had he for doing so?'

'Also we are still looking for the body of the Forestry Ranger; which I assume was also his handiwork; that makes you an accomplice to murder.' The man became visibly agitated:

'Now look here you can't pin that on me; that was his idea; he just shot the man in front of me without warning.' 'Unfortunately you did not inform the authorities;' said Cooper, 'which makes you an accessory after the fact and liable to be judged alongside your boss.'

The driver took out a cigarette and his hand was shaking so badly that Cooper had to hold it while he lit up.

His Brief leaned over and whispered something and the man nodded eagerly.

'My client has agreed to help you with your enquiries;' said the Brief. "

'Very wise if I may say so;' said Cooper, 'otherwise he would be looking at a very long sentence.'

The driver made a statement which Wearmouth took down and got him to sign; in it he admitted that he had set Von Richter down at a small boarding house in Queensferry before being dismissed.

Cooper was cock a hoop and rang Edinburgh 'Nick'with the news of Von Richter's whereabouts; they in turn sent several police cars to the address only to find they had missed him by three hours! Mrs Macenzie was bemused by this turn of events and told the police that her 'gentleman' had hired a car and gone sight seeing; unfortunately she knew not where. An APB was put out with a description of the hire car. Cooper was on the next train to Edinburgh, he was determined to be in at the kill.

CHAPTER NINETY SIX

Kossov awoke with a start in the Municipal Hospital; at first he thought he had gone blind, but on further scrutiny he discovered that his face and arms were bandaged and he had a drip in his right arm.

A nurse bustled into the room; noticed he was awake and said, 'good, I can tell the doctor that it will be alright for the police to come and interview you.'

'Why do they want to see me?' asked Kossov confusedly.

"Don't you remember the explosion?' said the nurse.

'I don't remember anything at the moment;' replied Kossov. 'Well you can explain it to the doctor; he'll be coming to examine you later,' she said turning on her heel and walking out of the room.

Kossov groaned; the last thing he needed was to be interrogated by the Argentinean Police, especially with their 'bedside manner.'

In his present state of mind he was liable to say things he would regret; he had to get out of here. He pulled the drip out of his arm and rolled out of bed; Picking himself up he realised that he was as weak as a kitten. Finding his clothes hanging in a cupboard he managed to dress himself. Carefully he looked out into the corridor; there was no one about. He noticed the lift doors were open and he slipped inside and pressed the button for the basement.

CHAPTER NINETY SEVEN

Von Richter drove slowly across the Forth road bridge; it had only just opened in the September of the previous year. He could not help admiring this engineering achievement; the British were to be congratulated for accomplishing this masterpiece. He glanced down at the great expanse of water below; when he had achieved his task all this would belong to the German people. Continuing up the A9 he came to the sign for Loch Leven and he turned onto the approach road. Avoiding the Municipal car park he drove on by the side of the loch till he found a suitable place to hide the car.
There was a small track that led to the water and began following it down.

As he progressed he heard voices ahead; quickly taking refuge in the bracken he listened to the conversation. Apparently it was between two policemen.

'It was hard luck that the squad arrived too late at Queensferry.' said one. 'Aye Angus we woud'ne be havin te patrol the banks o the Loch the noo.' responded the second.

Von Richter's blood ran cold; they must have caught the driver and he had been betrayed.

'If he's got ony sense he'll be a long way frae here,' commented the first officer.

'He'll stand a better chance if he keeps gayen north, there's nay so mony 'Bobbies' in the Heilands.'

The fugitive took the policeman's advice and carefully stole back to where he had left the car. His mind was in turmoil; he should have eliminated the driver instead of letting him go.

CHAPTER NINETY EIGHT

Next day Edinburgh police received a report of a sighting of the Hire car driven by Von Richter; it was heading towards Perth. Cooper commandeered a car and made for the M9; he had to intercept the man before he could carry out his mad scheme. The fact of the matter was that Von Richter was spoiled for choice as far as stretches of water were concerned in the Highlands. Cooper knew it was going to be like looking for a needle in a haystack. He had however spoken to Tony Hart before departing and Tony had promised to request aerial surveillance from RAF Lossiemouth, he reached Perth and called in at the local Police station. The Constable who had reported the sighting had been visiting a farmer who had complained about someone letting his sheep out when he noticed the car traveling in the opposite direction towards the city. Unfortunately it was only when he was returning to the station that he realised what he had seen. Cooper hit the road again and sped towards Pitlochry hoping against hope that he would not be too late. He reached the old Highland town in mid afternoon and slowly drove through the main street looking for a blue Cortina without success. Obviously the place was too full of tourists for Von Richter to chance dropping his deadly virus into the reservoir. Driving on he reached Dlalwinnie where to his horror the road divided; one carrying on to Inverness and the other towards Glencoe.

CHAPTER NINETY NINE

Kossov stumbled out into the street and the harsh light of day; he was still groggy from the blast of the bomb that the Teutonic Warriors had left in his house, but he focused on getting as far away from the hospital as possible. He had no money so he tried his luck at thumbing a lift and eventually a lorry driver took pity on him and stopped. He managed to climb into the cab; as the lorry pulled away the driver asked him where he was heading and he said;

'Wherever you're going will do.'

'Had a row with the missus?' laughed the driver.

'Something like that.' Answered Kossov wearily; at the moment he wanted to be as far from Buenos Aires as he could get. He had to somehow contact a member of his group who could take him in; he dared not go back to what was left of his house; as no doubt it would be under surveillance.

He borrowed enough from the driver to make a phone call and the driver dropped him off in a small village where he put a call through to Isaac; Mossad's book keeper. He explained what had happened and asked if Isaac could pick him up.

Isaac replied that he would get his wife to mind the shop and he would come over in his van. Isaac was a watch maker by trade and very useful in bomb making as well. He had worked for the Zionist cause for many years and was a reliable fellow.

Simon waited impatiently by the roadside until an hour later he espied Isaac's old Renault van coming down the road. The van pulled up and Isaac leaned over and opened the passenger door; Kossov climbed stiffly in, it had seemed a long time since quitting the Hospital. He was soon asleep as they made their way back to the city. Isaac glanced at the sleeping figure and shook his head; his leader looked all in, obviously the ordeal of the attempt on his life had pretty well drained him of his usual vitality.

CHAPTER ONE HUNDRED

Cooper had decided to take the road to Fort William via
Glencoe as it was less likely that Von Richter would take the
busier road to Inverness. He knew it was a gamble, but it
seemed the more likely choice. As he made his way up the
pass of Brander the terrain became wilder and the atmosphere
more oppressive; all sorts of murderous deeds had been
perpetrated around here in the turbulent histories of the
Highlands. He came into Glencoe just as the rain started again
adding to the malevolent brooding effect of the dark
mountains. He shuddered involuntarily; this was where the
Campbels had massacred the Macdonalds after inviting them to
a feast; an act of treachery long remembered in Scottish
memory. He was tired; it seemed an age since he had left
Edinburgh on this wild pursuit and he needed food and a rest.
He arrived in the main street of Fort William just as dusk was
falling; the rain on the windscreen distorting the street lights
into orange blobs.

Parking up he hurried into a café and ordered coffee and a
plate of beans on toast. When it arrived he struck up a
conversation with the owner,
'Do you happen to remember a blue Cortina coming
through here about two hours ago?' The man rubbed his
nose reflectively and answered; 'Ah seem to remember a
foreign gentleman comin in for a sandwich aboot that

time, aye his car was blue right enough.' 'He was askin aboot the lochs around here and whether the supplied the watter the noo.'

'Can you direct me to the nearest one?' asked Cooper excitedly.

The man gave him directions and Cooper hurriedly ate his beans and drank his coffee.

Producing his Warrant Card he told the man to ring the local police and inform them that the man he was chasing was wanted for murder and could they come out to the loch? Leaving the bemused man with his mouth open he dashed out into the rain and drove into the night.

CHAPTER ONE HUNDRED AND ONE

Cooper squinted through the rain soaked windscreen as he drove towards Gairlochy, it had not stopped since he had arrived in Fort William and he was beginning to feel the effects of the long pursuit. To add to his problems this was a typical Highland road; narrow with passing places every so often, with the occasional sheep using it as a sleeping place. He was making for Loch Lochy, which the Café owner had informed him was the local reservoir, would he be in time? The man had a two hour start on him and may have already thrown the Mn43 into the Loch. He tried not to think about that scenario as he pressed on towards his destination, soon coming into the small village of Clunes alongside the Loch. He drove slowly through the deserted street looking for the blue Cortina, but there was no sign of it. The Forest of Clunes was coming up with imposing mountains looming behind rising up over 2900 feet. He began to despair of finding Von Richter in the rain and the dark, but he had to stop the man if humanly possible. His headlights caught the rear end of a car parked amongst the trees on the verge; it was blue. Cooper stopped the car and grabbing his flashlight from the glove compartment, jumped out of the car and ran over to the parked vehicle. Sure enough it was the one he was looking for; but there was no sign of the occupant. Fortunately the ground was sodden with the rain and his torch showed tracks going into the forest' he set off following the trail, hoping against hope that he was not too late.

CHAPTER ONE HUNDRED AND TWO

Isaac's wife, a homely body, made Kossov welcome. She bustled about making him comfortable and brought him a bowl of Loxion soup. The hot chicken flavoured liquid warmed him and he began to feel better. After a cup of black coffee he began to feel almost human.

He thanked Miriam profusely and turning to Isaac said; 'could we go somewhere secure? I need to talk to you about what needs to be done.' Isaac nodded and ushered him into his small workshop at the back of the house.

'I need to contact Tel Aviv and inform them of the situation;' said Kossov; 'The Nazis are determined to wipe us out and the local regime is hardly likely to help us.'

'We are always being moved on in this world;' remarked Isaac sadly, whose family had fled from Russia to escape the pogroms many years before.

Kossov picked up the phone and got through to Mossad headquarters; after a lengthy conversation he replaced the receiver and looked across at his friend.

'I have been recalled to Israel Isaac; it seems they want a full report and I have to be on a plane tonight.'

'What will happen to the rest of us?' asked Isaac concernedly.

Kossov put his hands on Isaac's shoulders and looked directly in his face; 'old friend I'm afraid it's a case of every man for himself; you must make arrangements to get across the border and when you are settled get in touch with Headquarters and they will see to your needs.'

'Contact as many of the Group as you can and warn them to go.' Impulsively he embraced Isaac and bade him farewell.

He was soon in a taxi heading for the airport where he picked up a flight ticket left at the reception desk and made for the waiting area. Kossov was unaware of the man in a long black leather coat, close cropped hair and an unsightly scar running down his right cheek, sitting at the counter of the snack bar reading a paper.

As he passed the man folded his paper and followed Kossov towards the lift to the check in floor. As the doors of the lift opened on the 2nd floor a woman screamed as she saw Kossov's body, the assassin pushed past her and made for the fire exit. As he ran down the stairs he unscrewed the silencer from the Walther PPK automatic, slipping them into the copious pockets of his coat. A white Mercedes was parked outside with its engine running, he slipped into the passenger seat as it pulled away and joined the motorway.

CHAPTER ONE HUNDRED AND THREE

The rain was running down his face as Von Richter struggled through the boggy terrain; "Damn this pestilential weather he thought. He felt the container of Mn43 in is jacket pocket, yes it was still there and soon he would throw it into the Loch and Operation Phoenix would be under way, He came into a clearing beside the water and took out the container, removing the phials; he took off the top of the first one and threw it as far as he could into the water, then a second and a third. As he was about to throw the next he heard a shout behind him; turning he saw a figure struggling through the mire towards him. He pulled out his gun and loosed off a couple of shots in the direction of the approaching figure, who dived to the ground and rolled behind a tree. Von Richter threw the box containing the remaining phials into the water and made for the trees away from the loch. Now he was climbing uphill; every so often he glanced behind him to see if he was still being pursued. Twice he glimpsed a figure flitting between the trees behind him causing him to fire two more shots; there were three rounds left on the clip and it was his last, he would have to save them for a more opportune moment to rid himself of this threat. He came out of the tree line into open ground where the silhouette of the mighty mountains just showed against the dark sky. Here was the place to rid himself of antagonist, whoever he was. Pulling his sodden coat around him he followed the bed of a swollen

CHAPTER ONE HUNDRED AND SIX

Below him Cooper glimpsed lights moving towards the mountain; he guessed it was the local police force coming to assist him. Unfortunately it would take considerable time for them to reach the area where he was now climbing. The terrain was becoming steeper and more difficult to traverse; the wind driven rain restricted his vision and made the ground treacherous under foot. However he was gaining on his quarry and now had him in plain sight. This was obvious also to Von Richter as he loosed off another shot in Cooper's direction and shouting something unintelligible which was snatched away in the wind. The German was now nearly at the end of his tether physically when he noticed what looked like another pathway to his right; making for it he found the going easier and the surface smoother. As he stumbled along he noticed it was becoming narrower; he looked back and saw his pursucr was still behind him. He had only one bullet left; turning he took careful aim and fired. Cooper spun round and fell; Von Richter's heart leapt, he had won; the enemy was vanquished, there was nothing now to prevent his escape, his spirits rose giving him new momentum. Hurrying round a bend he was brought to a sudden stop; there had been a rock fall and a large section of the path was gone. He wearily retraced his step to the place where Cooper had fallen his heart gave a leap; there was no body in sight. He glanced wildly about him, but he could see no sign of his adversary.

A feeling of impending doom began to settle in his mind; was the man still alive and capable of preventing him from fulfilling his destiny? As he continued along the path with the rain causing him to screw up his eyes; he saw something looming out of the darkness. A figure was confronting him, standing motionless with the wind flapping it's clothing, making it look even more terrifying; one arm hanging uselessly by it's side, the other raised and pointing directly at Von Richter; was this the Angel of Death? The words came clearly despite the wind; 'you are under arrest Von Richter for the murder of innocent people in the United Kingdom and many other countries; anything you say will be taken down and may be used in evidence against you in a Court of Law.'

Von Richter saw that it was indeed Cooper and he was injured. 'I despise your law and everything your country stands for; you had your chance in 1939 to join the Great Plan of our beloved Fuhrer, but your blind stupidity overwhelmed your common sense under the reckless leadership of Winston Churchill.' As he was speaking he was edging ever closer to Cooper; suddenly, making a leap, he grabbed him and endeavoured to throw him over the side of the mountain. 'Cooper was at a disadvantage as the shot had hit his shoulder rendering his left arm useless. Nevertheless he fought with all his might as the two combatants got ever nearer to the edge.

Von Richter's feet slipped from under him and he slid over the edge, nearly taking Cooper with him. He let go and scrabbled desperately at the wet ground in order to prevent his fall; 'Helfen Mich!' he screamed as his hands slid inexorably towards the brink. Cooper grabbed the wretched man's right hand with his good one, but to no avail as it slipped out of his grip. With a final despairing scream Von Richter disappeared as he hurtled down the mountain side. The police search party stream towards the foothills.

CHAPTER ONE HUNDRED AND FOUR

Cooper stumbled along the pathway towards a clearing where he saw Von Richter throwing something into the water; 'God' he was already contaminating the Loch He shouted to him to stop and the man pulled a gun and shot at him. He dropped to the floor and got behind a tree, this was something he hadn't bargained for; he wondered how many shots the German had left. Cautiously peering around the tree he perceived that Von Richter was now making his way up a steep path away from the loch. Cooper vowed to himself that however he could achieve he would arrest the man and bring him to Justice; but just how he was going to do it was not clear at this moment. He followed at a safe distance, using the trees as a shield, but even so Von Richter loosed off two more shots as they toiled up the steep path towards the mountains. It was hard to keep the figure of his quarry in sight in this awful weather and several times Cooper had to stop and squint into the driving rain before he could spot him. However, fortunately Cooper realised that Von Richter was following the course of a stream, so he followed suit as they progressed into the mountains. It was obvious to Cooper his main aim of stopping Von Richter carrying out his fiendish plan had failed and it was impossible to imagine the consequences of this act of madness. Even the fact that an antidote had been found was no comfort, as it had to be produced in sufficient quantities to stop the plague spreading like wildfire; millions of innocent people were going to die; including his little family. That thought hit him like a bolt from the blue and his anger began to build in him as he stumbled after this self appointed Angel of Death.

CHAPTER ONE HUNDRED AND FIVE

Von Richter was tiring as he toiled up the side of Choire Gairth, the highest of the local peaks; it was being cruelly brought home to him that he was no longer a fit man. The terrain was changing as well; he was now clambering over a mixture of loose scree and large rocks dotted with stunted trees. He found keeping his footing more and more difficult and clung to any bush or tree in his path. The rain was now more intense and the wind was rising, causing the raindrops to sting his face. His mind went back to those days when he had led his squad through the Russian lines to freedom despite the terrible hardships and winter weather; he had succeeded then and he was going to now. He would live to see the new Germany rise from the ashes of World War Two to its rightful place as the Master Race in charge of the whole world. He could almost hear the sound of a Military band playing patriotic tunes coming through the gusty blasts of the wind as his uncertain steps led him ever higher up the mountain.

Cooper was slowly gaining on his quarry, being a younger and fitter man his progress was more sure, driven by an iron will and mounting anger at this arrogant madman. How dare he decide who was going to live and who was going to die, for a warped sense of the importance of his country's position in the world? Everyone had the right to determine their own destiny; in his opinion it was the right of all men that they should be free. He quickened his pace despite the driving rain that stung his face into the wild dark night.

discovered Cooper lying on the path where Von Richter had plunged to his death. They had heard the scream as he fell and this had helped them to pinpoint where Cooper might be. They carefully carried him down the mountain to a waiting ambulance, where medics stemmed his bleeding and he was taken to the local Cottage Hospital where he was tended by a doctor; an hour later he was tucked up in bed and fast asleep.

When he awoke he found Tony sitting on the bed munching his grapes.

'Hallo sport how are you feeling?' he asked.

'As if I've been run over by a train;' Cooper responded,'Look Tony why aren't you out there stopping Mn43 doing its work?'

Tony took some more grapes out of the bag and said; 'as a matter of fact there is some good news on that front.' 'Our friends at Portland Down discovered that the virus is temperature sensitive and has mutated in to a form of flu so apart from giving a lot of people runny noses it's harmless.'

Cooper began to laugh; 'the Nazi's went to all that trouble to give people colds?' 'I'll bet the tissue manufacturers have made a killing.'

Tony looked at his watch; 'Get well sport, I've got to leave for Whitehall for a de-briefing and the Air Force have kindly put a helicopter at my disposal, 'so saying he put the empty bag on the bedside cabinet and with a cheery wave he was gone.

CHAPTER ONE HUNDRED AND SEVEN

Two days later Cooper was discharged with his left arm in a sling and was driven back to Newcastle. He just had time to renew his acquaintance with Wearmouth and his team before being sent for by Superintendent Anderson. On arriving at his office Anderson came round the desk and shook Cooper's hand vigorously, 'Well done Detective Sergeant, it has been a privilege working with ye.' he boomed. 'I couldn't have managed without the help of Inspector Wearmouth and his men sir;' responded Cooper modestly.

'Aye, weel there's something in that;' said Anderson swelling with pride, 'they're a good team right enough.' Returning to his desk he opened the top drawer and produced a hip flask and two tumblers; carefully pouring out two shots of double malt whisky. 'Ye'll tak wee dram wi me will ye the noo Cooper te celebrate a successful conclusion te the case?' Cooper required no second bidding, raising his glass he cried 'Slancha va.' and drained his glass.

Anderson nearly choked and then laughing said; 'by God we'll mak a Scotsman o ye yet; but your accent l' need a bit o work.'

He pressed Cooper to have another for the road, but, looking at his watch he excused himself as the train for Birmingham was due very shortly and he was itching to get home and see his family.

Anderson shook his hand again and said; 'if you're ever in Newcastle again Cooper dinna hesitate te come and see us.'

A police car took him to the station where he boarded the train shortly before it pulled out of the station. Settling back in his seat he wondered how Sheila had taken the news of his injury; that there would be an inquest when he arrived home was not in doubt. Mind you she had already been subjected to her father being posted all over the Empire; so she was most likely conditioned to the vagaries of a policeman's life, but probably drew the line at her husband being shot.

CHAPTER ONE HUNDRED AND EIGHT

As the train drew into Norwich Thorpe station Cooper was already at the carriage door eager to get home and be with his family. However his joy turned to annoyance as he emerged from the station; someone had tipped off the Press and flash bulbs were going off in all directions. Reporters started shouting questions at him about his personal involvement in the death of Von Richter, as several microphones were thrust under his nose; God; even the BBC were involved.

Overwhelmed by this farrago he dashed over to the taxi rank, climbed into a cab and shouted to the driver; 'Get me the hell out of here will you.'

The cabby obliged, just catching the lights as they changed.

'Where to Mate,' he asked;

Cooper gave him his home address and settled back in his seat. The ambush by the press had unsettled him; he knew by experience that he would be hounded by the media without mercy until they had got every nuance out of the story. However his first duty was to his family, there were bridges to build with Sheila and he need to bond with Lawrence again in case he had forgotten who his daddy was. There would be a debrief at the Station and no doubt Grant would organise a Press Conference after that. The taxi drew up outside his house and he paid off the driver and ran up the path.

He banged on the front door with his good arm and it was opened immediately by Sheila, who had glimpsed the taxi arriving from the lounge window. '

'Hello stranger.' she said as he enfolded her in his good right arm and kissed her heartily

'Whoa boy;' she said, 'what will the neighbours think?'

'They're just jealous that they aren't getting any.' Said Cooper as he steered her into the hallway. 'Careful," she warned, 'small people are about who ask awkward questions about what grown ups get up to.'

On cue Lawrence appeared riding his trike and on seeing his daddy broke into a broad smile and collided with the wall.

'I see my son and heir's driving skills haven't improved.' Cooper remarked as he stooped and kissed his son.

Later as they sat on the sofa he related what had happened in Scotland and also the great news about the Teutonic Warrior's failure to carry out their dastardly plan. Sheila was concerned about his arm, but he reassured her that the damage wasn't permanent as the bullet had passed through the fleshy part and was healing normally. 'Well, just promise not to make a habit of it,' said Sheila; 'I don't want my husband coming home looking like a piece of Gruyere cheese.'

He kissed her tenderly and raised his eyes towards the ceiling; Sheila took the hint and they made their way towards the stairs.

www.ingramcontent.com/pod-product-compliance
Lightning Source LLC
LaVergne TN
LVHW051629080426
835511LV00016B/2258

*9 7 8 1 9 1 6 4 1 5 1 0 2 *